Hey Church, Stop Being Manipulated!

Dale Campfield

Dedication

To my Bride: Among all of the beautiful attributes that you possess, I appreciate most of all the love you have for God and the ways in which you express that love to everyone your path of life shares. You shall forever be, my best friend.

Acknowledgment

A special thank you to all of you who helped make this book possible, without you in my life I would not have been able to write it. Cathi (Butch), the most beautiful woman in the world; Cazi, Linzi and Iziah (Max), who have inspired me beyond measure; Dr. Badu Bediako, for opening up my eyes; Tim and Debbie Turton, for giving me a safe place to write; Justin (J-spot) Cain, for your artwork, time and Kingdom talents; Aunt Peg Delaney, Sharan Strub, Rick Campfield, Don Flannery, Artyce Homan, for your endless hours of editing; Steve and Sam Kline, for your Kingdom giving hearts; Ginny Campfield, for reminding me to know who I am; Rev. Jerral Campfield, for your example in how to love your wife as Christ loves the Church; to Elder Glen Homan, for your wisdom, love and knowledge of the Word which you have exemplified in my life; but most of all – to God Almighty, who has shown me His unconditional love in spite of my sinful ways.

Table of Contents

Forward
by Dr. Carl Morris

Dr. Carl Morris
Senior Pastor – Abundant Life Church
Florence, South Carolina

Dale,

Even just 40 pages in, I can already see how you are navigating through one of the most difficult subjects masterfully. You write from a place of genuine authenticity which will make it easy for the reader to receive the truth of your message, even those who don't know you personally.

I LOVE the techniques you have employed. . . . Famous Movie Quotes. . . . and ending the chapters with the recurring theme "OK, now it's time to GET REAL". A stroke of writing genius! If I didn't know better, I would think you've been writing bestselling books all your life!

I read your first manuscript *(Hey God, Is It Too Much to Ask)* in one sitting. But this one requires a slower pace in order to process the content of the message. That's a good thing. Heavy topic!

I am appreciating your personality reflected in this book. The Arrrggghhhs. The "OK Campfield, how many more are you going to cover. . .?".

You have spoken truth on a most difficult subject. I was convicted and forced to see how I have been blinded to my own capacity to manipulate and abuse people. The spirit of your writing makes the sharp truth you deliver palatable. I love you for speaking a heavy truth with such love.

I am going to use this as a resource. Your chapter on Church vs Kingdom mindset. . . . . . and the chapter on Characteristics of a Religious Spirit. . . . will be a tremendous asset to any pastor that teaches on the subject.

Honestly, this book is so different from your first. This one has to be digested differently. Your second book transcends your first, which is a compliment to an author who is still in the early stages of building his body of work. This book will set some people free while upsetting others who reject the truth.

An excellent job, my friend. I fully expect this to quickly become a classic study on the subject of spiritual authority, manipulation, and abuse.

Carl

Introduction

I am a recovering spiritual manipulator as well as a victim of spiritual manipulation. I've done and experienced both. And, chances are, if you have been a member of a Church for any length of time, you have too. I've found that spiritual manipulation and abuse surfaces in an assortment of ways: sometimes it is flagrantly in your face, while at other times it's subtly behind your back. It varies from the relatively benign to the lethally toxic, and it usually stems from a misuse of ecclesiastical authority by religious leaders toward members within a group or church of people perceived with "lesser status". Regardless of the degree of manipulation and abuse, it is and always will be harmful.[1] Many people have walked away not only from the Church due to abuse, but have walked away from God as well.

As you read this book, keep in mind that power is always at the source of every conflict, every control mechanism and every abuse issue. Power is at the heart of parent-child conflict, husband-wife arguments, and just about every war that has been fought.

At just a few weeks old babies lying in their cribs, will raise their arms to their parents. We see that as communication and it is. It says, "Meet my needs." In this case, the powerless is using the only method he or she has to ask one more powerful to meet his or her needs. We all learn how to do this. And we willingly meet loved ones' needs because we love them. So when does this move from love to abuse, from service to power grabbing, from a heart of concern for others to manipulation?

Manipulation vs. Motivation

While attending a Cincinnati Reds baseball game with my kids, the sounds of the organ echoed through Great American Ball Park as the organist played the "Charge!" theme. One can hear it now, "do do do do - do doooooo – CHARGE!" The music excited the crowd as we cheered the home team on to victory.

About half way through the game my daughter turned to me and asked, "Dad, is there a difference between manipulation and motivation?" My response, "Absolutely." On that day, the organist played the music in hopes to motivate the crowd to cheer the team on. The organist did not play with the motive, "Don't I sound good?" The motive was, "Doesn't our team look good?!" It was the desire of that musician for the team to end the game with one more victory under their belt; as opposed to him/her receiving the glory.

As the organist played, could one see this as a form of manipulation, trying to manipulate the crowd into a response? Yes, in a sense. However, the answer truly lies in the *motivation* of the one playing the music. **If the motivating factor of someone is to bring attention to himself or herself to enhance their popularity, to bring attention to themselves for what they do or who they are, then I consider that to be manipulation.**

Manipulation is persuading others to take an action that is primarily for your own benefit. It happens in the work place with bosses asking their employees to work overtime with no extra pay, to sell an inferior product at an inflated price so that they can make more money. It happens when a coach pushes his athletes beyond their own capabilities, causing injury to themselves, just so the coach can add a victory to his personal record.

Motivation occurs when you try to persuade others to take an action in their own best interest or in the interest of the greater population. This happens when a coach will push his athletes beyond their own capabilities but not past the breaking point. The desire is for the team to win, for *all* of them to look good.

I like what Zig Ziglar stated one time in his email newsletter, "Comparing motivation to manipulation is like comparing kindness to deceit. **The difference is the intent of the person.** Motivation will cause people to act out of free choice and desire, while manipulation often results in forced compliance. One is ethical and long-lasting; the other is unethical and temporary." [2]

Is it good for Christian leaders to motivate others? Absolutely. Is it okay for Christian leaders to manipulate others? Absolutely not.

You may agree to disagree – and that's okay

Many of my pastor, evangelist, prophet, missionary, and musician-type ministry friends might not appreciate this book. In fact, some of them might disagree with me completely. And to be honest with you, a few years ago I probably would have disagreed as well if someone told me I was spiritually abusing the Church! How dare they insinuate that I, a man of God, am abusing the Bride of Christ; that I'm causing harm to the Kingdom of God! How dare they! Well, I'm daring to speak this Truth now as the Holy Spirit leads me.

My wife's reaction after reading this book the first time was concern that people who did not know me personally would consider me an angry person. After 32+ years of marriage she knows me better than I might even know myself; she did not want anyone to regard me as an angry person since she does not see that in me.

I have to agree with her. I am not an angry person at all. I'm a very loving, genuine person and have a love for all people no matter their destination throughout life. God has given me a passion for souls that I take to heart dearly and never want to be thought of as being angry.

Am I an angry person? No. However, am I angry that there have been a myriad of spiritual leaders in the past who have abused and manipulated innocent people? Yes. It cuts to the very core of my being to know that the Church has been and is currently suffering under the strong arms of those who abuse them, either knowingly or not.

If you sense a little anger within this author as you read this book, just know that it is a righteous anger from one who desires to see the Body of Christ stand up and be all that God has called them to be.

Objective of this Book

My whole objective in writing this book is to see the captives set free! In my opinion, the Church, meaning the Body of Christ, has been held captive for years under the manipulation and spiritual abuse of leaders attempting to control the Church. It's time for the Church to spread Her wings and fly! It's time for the Church to stop being manipulated. It's time for the Church to make an even greater impact for the Kingdom of God!

So to whom am I writing this book? I'm not writing it to the so-called clergy, the local pastor, missionary, prophet, evangelist, or anyone who leads others in a Church, ministry, or religious organization. This book is addressed, as you'll notice in the title, to *the Church*. I'll be talking a lot about the clergy, Church leaders and those in spiritual authority; but the book is not for them. (Though I hope they read it.)

With that being said, keep in mind that this writing is in no way meant to come against any individual person, organization, religious institution or ministry. I respect you for what you do and respect the Call of God upon your life and the vision to which God has called each of you. In no way do I want to come across as a "know-it-all" in this subject. I'm just a fellow servant who has, sadly, fallen into the common trap of manipulating God's people, the Church.

Remember, you *are* the Church. You don't *go* to Church. It's impossible to go to something that you are. The Church is not a building or location where we go to celebrate our faith in Jesus Christ. The Church is who we are; men and women, boys and girls, people of all races and nationalities who commonly refer to Jesus Christ as their Lord. We are followers, disciples of Jesus, The Church.

I am amazed that nowhere in the New Testament do we find the terms "church" (ekklesia), "temple", or "house of God" used to define a building. Frank Viola states, *"To the ears of a first-century Christian, calling an ekklesia (church) a building would have been like calling your wife a condominium or your mother a skyscraper!"* [3]

According to Viola, the first recorded use of the word *"ekklesia"* to refer to a Christian meeting place was penned around AD 190 by Clement of Alexandria (150-215). Clement was also the first person to use the phrase "go to church", which would have been a foreign thought to the first-century believers. Throughout the New Testament, *"ekklesia"* always refers to an assembly of people, not a place. *"Ekklesia"*, in every one of the 114 appearances in the New Testament, refers to an assembly of people. The English word "church" is derived from the Greek word *"kuriakon"*, which means "belonging to the Lord." In time, it took on the meaning of "God's house" and referred to as a building. [4]

As I use the term "church" throughout this book, I will be referring to the church in two different contexts. When the word Church is capitalized, this will denote the Body of Christ, the Church. When the word church is in lower case, this will denote the old mindset that the church is a building that we attend once a week. For example, *"I go to church to worship God"* in comparison to *"I am the Church who worships God wherever I am."*

Though this topic of manipulation might be a tough message, I am compelled to share it because I believe that many of us, including myself, have exercised our so called spiritual authority over people for too long and it must stop. It's time for spiritual leaders to stop manipulating the Church, and it's time for the Church to stop being manipulated. This type of "religious exploitation" is most easily identified when accompanied by overt manipulation or coercion.

However, it may arise in a less obvious, but no less harmful, fashion when employed by likeable, even lovable, and charismatic individuals. Parents may spiritually abuse children; husbands and wives may spiritually abuse and manipulate each other; pastors abuse members; board members abuse ministers; televangelists abuse supporters, and the lists goes on. All this is done in an attempt to advance their own self-interests over others in a religious context.

As you'll see through this book, I have found that a great deal of those who are manipulating others through spiritual abuse are often times not even aware of it. It is something they have done since the beginning stages of their ministries. A great number of us have grown up with the example taught by those before us regarding how to manipulate others and didn't even realize it was happening. Actually, I believe we are taught how to manipulate others in many of our Bible Colleges and Seminaries and do not even realize it is happening. It's become common practice in many religious institutions and organizations; an unspoken curriculum offered at every level of ministry training.

Though you will never see a class offered at the local Bible School called Manipulation 101, it's the spirit of manipulation that is taught and passed on throughout the generations of time past. We've pretty much adopted it into the fiber of the modern Church world and accepted it without reservation. Though we would be the first to say that it is not a part of who we are, in many cases it is exactly who we are.

Are we evil? No! Is the spirit of manipulation, control and abuse evil? Yes! Can we become evil if we continue to practice forms of manipulation, control and abuse? Absolutely. Is that our heart? Of course not! Do we want to change? Mmmm, maybe. I certainly do!

Sometimes it's easier just to carry on with the way we always do things. It's easier to stay in the present mode of operation and just go with what we think works. How's that working out for you? Is your ministry flourishing like you have never experienced before? Are you experiencing miracles left and right as you go along your journey of life? Are people knocking at your door to be a part of your Church, ministry, institution, program or religious organization? Could it be something is missing?

I pray that each of you will have an open mind as you read this book. Ask the Holy Spirit to enlighten you with the knowledge of knowing if you are manipulating others and if you are one who is currently being manipulated.

Who am I?

Good question. Let me briefly give you my background to let you know where I'm coming from. I grew up in the Assemblies of God denomination in a small but powerful Church on the Yakama Indian Reservation in Washington State. I love the Assemblies of God and shall always cherish the friendships I have made within our denomination.

I received my license and ordination through the Assemblies. I have since withdrawn from them and am now licensed and ordained with Evangel Fellowship International, known as EFI. EFI is a fellowship of Churches and ministers dedicated to developing and promoting unity and strength among its members. Membership with Evangel Fellowship International is a way of telling others that you have been recognized by a body of international leaders who have attested to your integrity, both personal and professional. I have found that membership with Evangel Fellowship International provides the fellowship and supportive strength many ministers and groups are seeking today. For me, it's like having all of the wonderful resources, helps, relationships, support, accountability and vision of a mainline denomination, without the baggage. I love EFI and recommend them to anyone who might be contemplating ordination, licensing or direction for ministry to get connected.

My bride Cathi (whom I affectionately call "Butch") and I began full time vocational ministry in 1983 in Montana at 23 years of age. By vocational ministry I mean we started to get paid a full time salary for being pastors. I'm aware that all of us are in the ministry in some way, shape or form, but some of us are paid to live out our callings and ministries. I'm thankful to the Lord for allowing us to get paid to do what we love the most. It's a joy and a complete blessing to live this type of life. Yes, it comes with its set of sorrows, heartaches, pain and struggles; but who doesn't have a job where those things aren't part of the experience? The beautiful thing about our job is the fact that we are blessed to experience the love, joy, peace, mercy, grace and wonder of God in the hearts and lives of people on a daily basis. We've got the best job in the world!

We started our ministry as youth, children's and worship pastors. We then moved back to Washington and finally to Ohio to serve in the same capacity. We have been serving as the lead pastors of Eastgate Community Church in Cincinnati, Ohio since September of 2007. Together, we co-pastor a Church of 2.1 million people in the greater Cincinnati area. God has blessed us and we are excited about the future of the Body of Christ in Cincinnati.

You may be thinking, "Wow, a Church of 2.1 million people, that's awesome! You must really be successful!" The sad fact is that most of the time those in full time vocational ministry are considered successful by their peers if they have lots of people coming to their churches. If you have a lot of people, you must be successful. One of the things that used to bother me was while attending pastor meetings, someone would inevitably ask the question, "So how many people do you have coming to your church?", or "How many are you runnin'?" The question was posed to find out if I was successful or not and how that compared with their Church. It drove me crazy, and it still does! It leads to the whole ungodly environment of competition between Churches! I hated being asked that question. So, I stopped replying with "padded" numbers I used to make myself look good.

Over the years Butch and I have come to the absolute conclusion that there is only one Church and only one Body of Christ; we just happen to be one of the Shepherds God has raised up and called to walk within the Body. We're one of a multitude of Shepherds called "pastors" around the globe. Thus we've adopted the truism that even as there are about 2.1 million people in the greater Cincinnati area, we co-pastor these people with a lot of great pastors in the city. It's a big Church! A lot of people! 2.1 million! (According to *Wikipedia* [5], the Cincinnati-Northern Kentucky metropolitan area [aka Greater Cincinnati] is a metropolitan area that includes counties in the U.S. states of Ohio, Kentucky and Indiana, centered around the city of Cincinnati, Ohio. The United States Census defines the metropolitan area as the Cincinnati-Middletown Metropolitan Statistical Area [MSA]. As of the 2010 census, the MSA had a population of 2,130,151.)

How does that work?

In order to co-pastor a Church of this size, we have had to break it down into smaller groups. We have multiple sites around the city where people come to worship God; some people come on Saturdays, others on Sunday and some on the other days of the week. As well, we all have some slightly different doctrines to which we adhere, demonstrating love and respect for others while worshipping the same God in Heaven, our Lord and Savior Jesus

Christ. We have different buildings, but one God. We have different denominations, but we are one Church! We have different doctrines, but we collectively are the Body of Christ, *the Church*! Thus, we co-pastor a Church of 2.1 million people! Keep in mind that there are a great number of souls in our community that do not yet have a relationship with Jesus Christ, but they are coming!

Allow me to get back to who I am

Along the journey God has blessed Butch and I with four wonderful children, who are all currently serving in the body of Christ within their own respective ministries. We could not be more proud of them. Sadly, our daughter Cali passed away, but we are now blessed beyond measure with Cazi, Linzi, and Iziah (Max). You can learn more of our story in my book, *"Hey God, Is It Too Much to Ask?"* [6]

Hear my Heart; Why I Wrote this Book

Allow me to be candid; I find it heart breaking that for centuries of time, good hearted, Born Again, followers of Jesus Christ have assembled in their houses of celebration week after week being spiritually abused. It is heartbreaking for me to know that I have contributed to this abuse and am writing this hoping the trend of spiritual abuse will come to an end, and that the Church (again not a building we call church, but the Body of Christ called the Church) will arise and be who God has called them to be — to walk with the God given anointing that is upon their lives, with Kingdom Authority, carrying out their Kingdom Assignments.

I believe that as long as the Church allows herself to be spiritually manipulated by those in authority over them, she will never be able to walk in the fullness of her God-given potential, to make an eternal impact for the Kingdom of God on this earth, to fly.

With that being said, I don't believe that everyone, including myself, has intentionally gone about trying to be manipulative with the sole purpose of bringing about gain for our own lives. Yes, there are some that have, but most are probably not even aware they are doing it.

I believe most of us have fallen into what I call a Ministry Manipulation Trap, having a desire to please God and to walk in purity within our ministries; but over the years we have fallen into an abusive trap. And this trap of spiritual abuse has been handed down over the years along with our Spiritual Mantles.

I don't know about you, but I am increasingly alarmed at how pervasive the problem is and how often this spiritual manipulation is accompanied by egregious forms of legalism, the kind that shackles its victims with oppressively strict standards of performance. This kind of spiritual control, in the hands of an abuser, is often lethal to the heart and soul of the spiritually abused.

Thus I write this book...**Hey Church, Stop Being Manipulated!**

For Your Benefit. . .

At the end of each chapter I present a series of questions under the heading "Time to Get Real." This is your opportunity to "get real" in dealing with your own issues of spiritual manipulation.

There are a number of ways to ensure this exercise will be the most impactful for your life. Of course, you can answer the questions on your own, which is good; but in order to obtain an even greater impact I would suggest you "get real" in the midst of a small group of people within your own Church family. Even as the Bible tells us that "iron sharpens iron", this is your opportunity to sharpen one another in the Body to take on a greater awareness of spiritual manipulation and begin to conquer those areas of your life in which you might find yourself being one who manipulates others.

Consider adapting the following guidelines as you meet together. . .

(See "For Your Benefit" at the end of the book for greater clarity on these guidelines.)

1. Truth – Everyone in the group must be committed to honesty and truthfulness.
2. Trust – Everyone in the group must be willing to trust each other.
3. Time – Everyone in the group must be respectful of each other's time.

Also. . .

You'll notice throughout the book I make reference to and quote a few movies from the past. This is for the readers who have enjoyed a few movies in their lifetime and may make the connection with the quotes that are given. If you don't enjoy or even attend movies, just skip right over them. But chances are, most of the movie quotes will trigger something in your past, as many of them have become a part of the culture, which we now live.

Okay. . . let's get on with the book.

Chapter 1

"A True Story"

"A True Story"

*A*llow me to share a true story with you with the blessings of my Pastor friends in Africa.

The Holy Spirit profoundly prompted me to write this book during a trip to Africa in May of 2012 where I was honored to officiate the funeral of the late Apostle Gabriel Bediako, brother to our missionary Dr. Badu Bediako in Kojokrom, Ghana. Kojokrom is about a five-hour drive into the bush country from Accra. I've been there on many occasions and enjoy the African way of life. I have many friends there who I will cherish forever.

Having a friend forever reminds me of this movie quote. . .

Famous Movie Quote:

2003 THE LORD OF THE RINGS: THE RETURN OF THE KING [1]

[Sam and Frodo both are overcome by exhaustion]
Sam: *"Do you remember the Shire, Mr. Frodo? It'll be spring soon. And the orchards will be in blossom. And the birds will be nesting in the hazel thicket. And they'll be sowing*

*the summer barley in the lower fields. . . and eating the first
of the strawberries with cream. Do you remember the taste of
strawberries?*

Frodo: "No, Sam. I can't recall the taste of food. . . nor the
sound of water. . . nor the touch of grass. I'm. . . naked in the
dark, with nothing, no veil. . . between me. . . and the wheel of
fire! I can see him. . . with my waking eyes!"

Sam: "Then let us be rid of it. . . once and for all! Come
on, Mr. Frodo. I can't carry it for you. . . but I can carry you!"

The day before I left Ghana to come home I was to minister at
a local Church in Accra. My friend, interpreter and man of God,
Pastor Kobi, picked me up in the morning to visit a pastor friend
of Kobi's Church. We arrived late. When we got there, the king
asked me to sit at his throne. Errr, I'm sorry, I mean the pastor
asked me to sit on his comfy cozy couch that was reserved for
the elite and in front of everyone. I invited Kobi to sit by me. He
hesitantly accepted telling me he wasn't normally allowed to do
so but would because I had asked him to.

Since we were late, the singing, worship, and dancing were
over; the pastor introduced me just minutes after sitting down.
I had no opportunity to meet or talk with him prior to the introduction. He apparently knew who I was, but I had no clue as to
who he was. Trying not to pass judgment on the pastor, I took
the platform. However, it was hard to ignore the uncomfortable
feelings I had had since the moment I laid eyes on him. I got the

"hee-bee-jee-bees" and red warning flags were popping up. The Holy Spirit was telling me to "beware". An indelible impression deep within my soul was screaming that something was wrong!

As I began the message I honored him as the pastor of this Church along with his family, honored Kobi and then I preached for almost an hour. The whole time I felt the hearts of the people, the Church, and their hunger for God. It was such a delight to minister to them. Following the message I gave a call for people to come forward, which everyone did. I prayed over them but did not feel compelled to lay hands on them. Thankfully I didn't.

Forgive my cynical attitude towards the local pastor. I'm sorry, but he really did give me the "creeps". As I preached, he sat on his couch pretty much not moving unless I referred to him. He sat there as if he were not interested in one thing I had to say outside of my acknowledgment of him. Now he may have just been having a bad day, but I don't think so.

After the altar experience I turned the microphone back over to the pastor. He had Kobi take up an offering, and then he took one up himself right after the one just taken. To my amazement he asked for those who would give 20 Ghana cedi's to come forward with their money. The Ghana cedi is the unit of currency of Ghana. The word "cedi" is derived from the Akan word for cowry shell (cowry shells were once used in Ghana as a form of currency). The new Ghana cedi was introduced on July 1, 2007 at a rate

32

equal to 10,000 old cedis. It was the highest-valued currency unit issued by sovereign countries in Africa in 2007.

Two people came forward, placed their 20 cedi's in the plate and received the prayer of a lifetime from the pastor, the prayer of his complete blessing, loud and exuberant with lots of emotion applied to the prayer. He prayed down heaven over those beautiful members of the Church. It was as if Elijah himself was there calling down fire from heaven. He gave it every ounce of strength he could to bless those wonderful souls!

He then had those come forward who wanted to give 15 cedi's, then 10, 5, 2 and 1 cedi with the prayers for each of these individuals becoming less powerful as the amounts decreased. The last call he gave, the 1 cedi amount, four families came forward to give; they received a completely lackluster, non-emotional, wimpy prayer of blessing. It was a prayer, but he sounded like the announcer who introduces the visiting team at a home game; a total lack of luster. My heart broke.

Such manipulation. Sad, sad, sad. Apparently in their Church if you give a lot, you get an enormous prayer of blessing spoken over you. If you give a little, you get a small blessing. Arrrggghhhhh!

The Prophet Moses, that's the title the pastor has given himself to be called by the Church, then started praying, and screaming at the people (emotionally manipulating them); forcefully knocking them down to the ground, pouring a bottle of oil over his own head then his two disciples (just drumming up the emotion of these innocent people, The Church). I wept in my spirit.

I felt compelled to grab my camera and take some pictures of this travesty. As I took them, I almost got the feeling that the pastor was putting on a show for my camera. Suddenly the batteries ran out. I put the camera away, but he continued with his antics. So apparently this was nothing new. It seemed to be "business as usual."

Sadly, there was nothing I could do about this abuse. I wanted to stop him but I could not. Kobi said this is the "African cultural way of ministry" for this guy, to which I say hog wash! Don't get me wrong, I respect and honor the culture wherever I go, at all times. I've been in numerous countries around the world for over 25 years and have experienced a great number of Church cultures. But this was not a Kingdom-of-God thing. This was an old church mindset that says the pastor can do whatever he wants to the sheep as long as he gets the response he is looking for; and it's wrong, no matter what culture you may be in.

The biggest error I felt happening in this African Church culture that morning was the elevating of the local pastor above everyone else; and the pastor himself was the one that dictated his elevation. It's wrong. It's idolatry. It's pride. It's sickening. And sadly enough, you don't have to go to a foreign country to experience this type of self-elevating control and power; it's happening in every Church culture in every nation around the world! I've experienced it first hand in Russia, Mexico, Guatemala, Greece, Romania, Jordan, Latvia, the Philippines and the United States of America! Get this. . . I firmly believe that God doesn't love pastors, teachers, prophets, etc. anymore than anyone else. **He loves the Church!** So this type of self-elevation and power-driven nonsense is exactly that, nonsense!

There are too many pastors and local spiritual leaders within the Church that elevate themselves above the people. Just as sad is the fact that a great majority of those in the Church are letting it happen by propping them up and elevating them to this place themselves. The leaders are manipulating the Church and the Church is letting it happen!

Arrrggghhhhh! Can you tell I'm upset?

Anyway, back to the true story. After the show, errr, I mean service, they took me into a side room to await the presence of Moses. His throne was in the middle of a side wall with a chair on each side for his disciples. I almost sat in one of those chairs until Kobi had me move, so Kobi and I both sat across from the throne.

Moses came in, very humble and quiet, seeming like a nice, meek, humble guy now. He sweetly had his disciples serve us cold water and drinks. In a soft beautiful tone he thanked me for preaching and said it was wonderful. He said that I am always invited to preach behind his pulpit whenever I'm in Accra. He rolled out the red carpet of honor to me. He gave me accolade after accolade.

I felt like the enemy was trying to seduce and pull me in.

I was polite and thanked him and said, "You have a great Church here, the people." I don't think he heard the "people" part. He just heard the "you have a great church here" part. We chatted a bit longer as I attempted to get Kobi to get me out of there.

Our missionary and host, Dr. Badu called on the cell phone, thankfully, interrupting our conversation. He asked where we were. He had bought lunch for me and was awaiting my arrival back at the hotel. Glory! My ticket out!

As I shook Moses's hand to say good-bye, ready to click his finger (which is the custom in Ghana) he stopped me to say he had a word of prophecy for me. Arrrggghhhhh. I was polite and listened, and it actually sounded great!

He said God was speaking through him as he said to me, "As I watched and listened to you share the word, (his disciple was translating for me) I saw that you began to glow with a white fire surrounding you. It flowed from your head down your body. As you stretched out your hands I saw oil dripping from your hands. God is about to release a new anointing upon you that will change the world. You will begin a ministry that will raise people from the dead. The things you have been praying for, God is going to bring to pass. Just wait on the Lord for three days and then He will begin to bless you."

Wow. . . . . What a prophecy! Who wouldn't want that, right? On the surface one would say, "Yes, I receive; bring it on!"

But I felt like a seducing, warm, demonic, manipulating spirit was trying to suck me into accepting him and buying into his ministry. I felt like he was trying to manipulate me into liking him. It's as if that evil presence were opening up its arms of control and inviting me to take part of the pleasures of "real ministry" - where the Church would look upon me with awe and respect and listen to my words with great anticipation. Also everyone would want me to be at their beck and call to lay hands upon them as they looked to me as "The man of God."

I said thank you and left as quickly as I could get my sandaled feet out the door, across the dirt, and into the taxi.

Now don't get me wrong. I'd love to have a ministry that raised people from the dead; and if that's God's plan then so be it. I won't stand in the way. But this was totally surreal and creepy from the very start. I felt somewhat like an innocent Church victim being spiritually abused by a member of the so-called clergy. My heart wept for his people, the real Church. They are innocent victims caught up in what they believe to be true, while trying to serve and worship God to the best of their ability.

Here's the thing; I don't feel the pastor himself was trying to be spiritually abusive, I think he was just doing what he's been taught. He has bought into the cultural lies of the church in Africa!

Even as I write this, please hear my heart. I want to make it perfectly clear that this is not the way it is for every Church in Africa! There are thousands of good, solid, biblically based Churches that are being pastored by the kindest of pastoral shepherds and spiritual leaders you'll meet anywhere around the world; and they're doing it in purity! I just happened to be at one that night that was a clear image of spiritual leaders manipulating the Church.

After getting back to the hotel, receiving my eggs and chips from Dr. Badu, I go into my room and turned on the T.V. What comes on?! An American televangelist, whipping the crowd into frenzy with his vocal and physical antics. I believe God was trying to tell me something. I believe God was trying to show me the error that is within a great number of local Church bodies around the world and that the manipulation **must stop** if we truly want to make an impact for God, changing the cultures in which we live.

<u>Time to Get Real. . .</u>

1. Define the differences between manipulation and motivation.
2. Do you think manipulation is a problem in the modern day Church world?
3. What abuses of power have you seen in your experience with Church life?

4. Have you ever been in a situation where you observed manipulation taking place but were unable to do anything about it? How did that make you feel?

5. If you could have done something about it, what would you have done?

6. Have you ever knowingly or unknowingly manipulated others in the Church?

Chapter 2

"I'm a Recovering Manipulator"

"I'm a Recovering Manipulator"

I have asked my bride and accountability partners to hold me accountable in the area of spiritual manipulation. I have asked them to tell me immediately if they see, read, hear, or feel in their hearts that I am manipulating people out of my position of spiritual authority over them. My heart would drop if I ever become like Pastor Moses. However, I must admit, I am a recovering manipulator and abuser of my authority. There seems to be an unspoken code of conduct in the "religious world" that would like for us pastors to believe that those who walk with spiritual authority have a right, as a minister of the gospel, to control others. Thus, unwittingly or not, we pressure, manipulate, persuade, cajole and threaten (always with creatively-wrenched scriptures and "pure" motives) the members of the Churches we "serve" with Herculean efforts to get our way or to impose our will over our subordinate flock.

I know I have manipulated innocent believers in the past to get a response out of them to feed my own ego or to get what I wanted; to which I have and do repent. I strive not to do this; but it has happened in the past and sadly, it continues to happen. I don't like it, but it happens. It's so easy to do. In fact we do it all the time. We all manipulate each other one way or another for the means of getting what we want.

For example, I say just the right thing in just the right way to get my bride to make me something special for dinner or to give me personal favors later in the day. My kids may say just the right thing at just the right time that will tug at my emotions, making me want to give them money to fulfill their evening plans. Manipulation happens all the time. It doesn't make it right, but we have learned throughout our lifetime how to manipulate others for our own gain.

As newborn babies, there is a natural instinct that children know how to get what they want right when they want it. They can get their parents to do just about anything with just the right cry, whine, or smile. I, for one, am one dad to whom my baby girls had me wrapped around their fingers when they were little, and still do!

Notice the simple manipulation in this conversation between Molly and Andy in the 2010 movie TOY STORY 3...

Famous Movie Quote:

2010 TOY STORY 3 [1]
[Andy is climbing up the ladder to the attic to put his toys away when Molly walks out of her room carrying a box]

Molly: *"Uh!"*

[a small heavy ball falls out of the box]

Andy: *"You need a hand?"*

Molly: *"I got it!"*

Andy: *"Here."*

[he puts the ball back and picks up the box]

Andy: *"So, you gonna miss me when I'm gone?"*

Molly: *"If I say no, do I still get your room?"*

[they walk down the stairs]

Andy: *"Nope."*

Molly: *"Then, yes, I'll miss you."*

Manipulation is always taking place. Have you ever been to a shopping market and exited the store with items you had no intention of buying when you went in? You had a goal in mind when you went in; you knew what you wanted and you had no intention of buying anything else. Then, when you got in there, you felt compelled to buy that extra item simply because the product display or free samples got you! Did you know there are people whose job it is to think of ways to manipulate you into buying their company's stuff? People are paid millions of dollars to market their wares hoping that you'll catch what they are offering and decide to buy it. It's manipulation.

Let me ask you this; have you ever walked out of a store, spent your total budget allotted for groceries that month only to find a little girl outside the door selling cookies? How can you resist that smile? How can you resist that cute little innocent being as she asks you if you want to buy a cookie? You don't have the extra money, but what do you do? You buy the cookie! You've been manipulated! Sure, it's for a good cause, but it's a form of manipulation either way you look at it.

It's a part of the fabric of our society. People manipulate others constantly. We manipulate others to pay for our lunches, take care of our kids, babysit our dogs, buy our homemade crafts, and take us to the movies!

<u>Time to Get Real. . .</u>

Let's be honest here.

1. How many of you manipulate others? In what ways do you manipulate them?
2. How often do you find yourself being manipulated on a daily basis?
3. Why do you think our society is so manipulative driven? Do you think it will ever change? Do you care?
4. Do you see manipulation as something negative or positive when used in "selling" something either in a Church setting or non-Church setting? Many sales positions are all about convincing customers to buy. Do you consider this to be manipulation? Do you think it's okay to do?

Chapter 3

"Biblical Manipulative Characters"

"Biblical Manipulative Characters"

*I*t's amazing to me to see how many examples we can find in God's Word of those who manipulated others for their own gain or reason. I've researched a number of them and find their stories unique.

In Biblical times, the sons of Samuel used their appointments as judges to take bribes, to pervert justice, and to accumulate personal wealth. Later on in time, God's choice for the position of Israel's first king, Saul, abused his power in an effort to kill the person chosen by Almighty God to be his successor - the little shepherd boy David! When David, himself, became king of Israel, he misused his power to commit adultery with Bathsheba, the wife of Uriah, one of his officers. Then, to make matters worse, King David conspired with others to have Uriah killed!

Many centuries later, we read about a little-known leader of the early church, Diotrephes, who misused his position of authority by denouncing others in order to elevate himself. He failed to recognize the fact that it is Almighty God who elevates and not mankind! Diotrophes was so protective of his own position that he would not even welcome the beloved Disciple/Apostle John, into his congregation. You can read all about it in 3 John 9-10.

In response to the actions of Diotrephes, the beloved Disciple/Apostle John, in 3 John 1:11 (NKJV), tells us: *"Beloved, do not imitate what is evil, but what is good. He who does good is of God, but he who does evil has not seen God."* Nobody knows how Diotrephes publicly explained his lack of hospitality, for the Bible does not reveal that to us. To be sure, however, the people of Almighty God must have wanted to know why he would not receive the Disciple/Apostle whom Jesus, the Christ, loved!

Perhaps, like many of those in Church leadership roles today, he simply assumed that after all he had done for the Church, he was entitled to unchallenged prominence within the Christian community. Sound familiar? Have you ever heard someone say, "You're sitting in my pew" or words to that effect?

There are many other examples in the Bible of people who tried to manipulate or control others. Let's look at a few more.

Potiphar's Wife

In this story we find Potiphar's wife trying to get Joseph to sleep with her in Genesis 39:6-13; a manipulation attempt that cuts to the heart of a man.

Joseph was one of twelve sons of Jacob. He was the boy who had dreams that one day his brothers and parents would bow down to him. This perceived arrogance didn't sit well with the brothers; so when they got their chance, they sold Joseph to slave traders who were going to Egypt. It was there Joseph became the slave of a man named Potiphar who was the captain of Pharaoh's guard. For years things weren't so bad for Joseph. He was respected by his master and quickly promoted head over almost everything in Potiphar's house. There was, of course, one thing that was off limits to Joseph: Potiphar's wife. Not that Joseph ever made advances on her. But when Potiphar's wife saw how handsome Joseph had become after years in their employ, she didn't beat around the bush but came right out and demanded, "Sleep with me!" This was a woman who was obviously used to getting her way and would manipulate her way into getting what she wanted. How did this man of God respond? He refused. He continued to refuse her and even declined to be in the same room. He saw the traps of manipulation and wanted nothing to do with her.

I pray the Church will see the traps the enemy has set before her and be able to run from them as well. Without a doubt, our enemy Satan has set familiar traps before each of us in an attempt to manipulate us into missing out on God's blessings, favor, and anointing. Let's be like Joseph and refuse the manipulative efforts of the enemy!

In Joseph's case, still the woman persisted, even as our enemies will. She was determined to make Joseph a conquest. She finally thought she had her chance when one day all the other servants were out of the house leaving her alone with Joseph. This time she grabbed his cloak and demanded, "Sleep with me!" What was poor Joseph to do? Consider his situation. Joseph had been sold into slavery by his brothers and given up for dead by his father. He must have been lonely and now here was someone who appreciated and wanted him. If he continued to reject Potiphar's wife, he might lose his job. Why not give in to this woman's demands? Plenty of other slaves had done worse things to keep their masters happy. Perhaps he could just flirt with her. Would that be so dangerous? Oh the games that the devil plays in our heads as manipulation plays itself out.

He continued his quest of denying this manipulative woman and was blessed for it in the long run. It wasn't an easy assignment, but God gave him the strength he needed and He'll strengthen you as well.

It reminds me of what Thor says in the Movie THOR in looking for strength. . .

Famous Movie Quote:

2011 Movie THOR[1]

[pointing to the name tag on the shirt he's about to put on]

Thor: *"What is this?"*

Jane Foster: *"Oh!"*

[she takes off the name tag from the T-shirt]

Jane Foster: *"My ex! Good with patience and bad with relationships! Uh. . .they're the only clothes I had that would fit you."*

Thor: *"They will suffice."*

[he walks away from her]

Jane Foster: *"You're welcome!"*

Thor: *"This mortal form has grown weak. I need sustenance!"*

Delilah

You remember Delilah don't you? I can still recall watching the movie made in 1949 by Cecil B. DeMille with actors; Hedy Lamarr, Victor Mature and George Sanders when Delilah manipulated her way into finding out Sampson's source of strength as found in Judges 16:5-21. This movie has now been colorized and still shows every now and then on the local television stations. They changed the way the movie looks, but they can't change the outcome of this story of manipulation.

The Valley of Sorek, where this story takes place, was half a mile from the brook Eshcol. It was from this valley that the spies brought grapes as a specimen of the fruit of the land of Canaan. Because it was a valley filled with vineyards, the valley also became famous for the best wine. It was to this place Samson decided to go every time he needed refreshment or sought pleasure.

If we are not careful, we will allow the blessings God provides for us to become a curse in that they will lead us into sin. How can that happen? Look at Proverbs 20:1 (NKJV), *"Wine is a mocker, strong drink is a brawler: and whosoever is led astray by it is not wise."*

The wine here not only speaks of partaking of fermented or alcoholic beverages, but it also speaks of anything in life that would become intoxicating to the point it would have the power to change your way of thinking and your way of acting. I've seen people lose their inhibitions in many ways through this form of manipulation. Some would lose it in their manner of speaking and begin to use profanity if the right circumstances arose. Some would lose their inhibitions in their manner of dress, just to be accepted as a part of the "in" crowd. Some would lose their inhibitions of honesty, quickly succumbing to lying or stealing, whether on their income taxes, or lying to get something they know they shouldn't have.

Samson sold out for a little pleasure and a little drink. Are we willing to sell out for that, or even less? *Thus says the LORD, "Let not the wise man glory in his wisdom, let not the mighty man glory in his might, nor let not the rich man glory in his riches: But let him that glories glory in this, that he understands and knows Me, that I am the LORD which exercise loving kindness, judgment, and righteousness, in the earth: for in these things I delight, says the LORD."* Jeremiah 9:23-24 (NKJV)

And so Samson, the mightiest man that ever walked the earth physically, decided to depend upon his own wits and his own strength. That, my friends, is a recipe for defeat in the making! **He set himself up to be manipulated and didn't even know it.**

So Delilah said to Samson, "Please tell me where your great strength lies, and with what you may be bound to afflict you." Judges 16:6 (NKJV)

Nothing in the world can make a man fail quicker than sexual pleasure and a beautiful woman. What God created and ordained for good, Satan has perverted; and man has devalued to the point it threatens to destroy mankind completely. Samson was caught in this web of passion and manipulation. In the beginning he could have walked away, but he chose not to. Now, the more he stayed involved with Delilah, the more impossible it was for him to break free. The bondage he faced was not just going to be green vines or new ropes, but it was a spiritual bondage and he was already tied up. The sins of the flesh were drawing the ropes ever tighter around his heart, "squeezing out" if you will, the Spirit of God that was with him. God cannot dwell where darkness reigns, and Samson's heart was going ever deeper into the powers of darkness.

One thing that really strikes me is that Samson didn't go into this temptation blindly. Delilah was honest with him right from the start. She didn't hide her true intentions. She actually began to manipulate him from the beginning; but Samson chose to ignore the signs of that manipulation as one who has a free will, which all of us do. He knew exactly what was at stake, and he still decided to play with fire. He thought he was stronger than anything that could be used against him. He presumed upon the grace and power of God.

And as the end of the story shows us, Samson is brought down emotionally, physically, and spiritually through the manipulation of Delilah. He does rise again at the end of his life to make an impact for God, but the price he paid in the process was a costly price indeed.

Naboth the Jezreelite and King Ahab

Let's look at the story of Naboth the Jezreelite and King Ahab. King Ahab went sulking about in hopes that his wife, Jezebel would get a vineyard for him that he desperately wanted as we read in 1 Kings 21:1-15.

Put yourself in the shoes of Naboth. One day you're out working in your vineyard, tending the vines, killing the bugs, pulling out the weeds and whatever else you do when you're tending a garden. Into your life arrives the King who makes you an offer you can't refuse, but you do.

What happens next is the King tells you he wants your vineyard to plant a vegetable garden. He offers to give you a better vineyard or whatever else you want. Just imagine Ty Pennington from the TV Show, *Extreme Makeover Home Edition* arrives at your door and says, "I love your house and I will trade you for a much nicer home or give you however much you want for it. You name the price!" The problem was, the vineyard had been in Naboth's family for longer than most people could remember. This was in all probability the plot given to his family hundreds of years before when the Israelites had first arrived into the Promised Land. To sell his birthright was against the law of God. So he didn't even think about it; he just told King Ahab no.

Well the King went home and climbed the "miff" tree, got all upset, and started whining. The King began to sulk. Poor king. It wasn't hard to notice he hadn't gotten his own way; he'd just gone in, thrown himself on his bed and stared at the wall. He wouldn't come out, not even for dinner. Some would say if the man won't come out for dinner, then he's got to be upset! While he's having fun at his own pity party, his wife Jezebel comes along and wants to know what's wrong. Ahab tells her in 1 Kings 21:6, *"I asked Naboth to sell me his vineyard or to trade it, and he refused!"* (You wonder why he needs a vineyard when he can produce that much "whine" with just his voice.)

It reminds me of a conversation between a whining Luke Skywalker and his Aunt Beru.

Famous Movie Quote:

1977 Movie STAR WARS - A NEW HOPE [2]

Aunt Beru: *"Where are you going?"*

[in a whiny toned response is]
Luke: *"Looks like I'm going nowhere. . . I'm gonna finish cleaning those droids."*

And you've got to love this scene of whining discontent from Luke Skywalker of the same movie. . .

[Referring to R2D2 and C3PO]
Uncle Owen: *"Luke! Take these two over to the garage will you? I want them cleaned up before dinner."*

Luke in a whiny voice: *"But I was going into Tosche Station to pick up some power converters."*

Uncle Owen: *"You can waste time with your friends when your chores are done. Now come on. Get to it."*

Luke: (Gasping for air) *"All right. Come on."*

[R2D2 whines.]

Now personally I love the response of the Queen because she says, "Aren't you the King of Israel?" And then she tells him, "Get out of bed and eat something! Don't worry, I'll get Naboth's vineyard for you." Manipulation. His whining worked. He got her to do what he wanted.

Martha

The story of Martha's appeal to Jesus to make Mary help her prepare a meal in Luke 10:38-42 is also a story about manipulation along with a myriad of other lessons. The story takes place in the village of Bethany, which is located just outside of Jerusalem. From what we can glean in this passage and in John chapters 11 and 12, Martha lived with her sister Mary and their later to-be-famous brother, Lazarus. It appears that Martha is a widow, for she is the head of the household. Here in the home of Martha, Mary, and Lazarus, Jesus and his disciples sit down for some relaxation away from the press of the crowds. Here is a home Jesus had been in many times, a place He knew He was loved and accepted. Both sisters are delighted to see Jesus; but as you will see, they express their enthusiasm in very different ways. In verse 38 we are told, *"Now it happened as they went that He entered a certain village; and a certain woman named Martha welcomed Him into her house. And she had a sister called Mary, who also sat at Jesus' feet and heard His word."*

People have varying temperaments; some are active always needing to be busy, never able to sit still. Others are thoughtful, willing to sit back and think things through. Martha is a very activity-oriented person; her sister appeared to be of the more thoughtful nature. I believe many times we have wrongly contrasted Martha and Mary, as though each Christian should make a choice to either be a worker like Martha or a worshipper like Mary. But in so doing I think we miss the point; the Lord wants each of us to imitate Mary in our worship and Martha in our work and to achieve balance in both areas.

Mary is content to sit at Jesus' feet, soaking up the Word and not "doing" anything. But her big sister, Martha was looking around at all the guests and saw the need to prepare a meal. Martha was obviously a great hostess; she got up and began to prepare food for Jesus and the entire group with Him. Martha looked and said to herself, "What a privilege to prepare a meal for the Master!" Mary on the other hand, would have said, "What a privilege to sit at the feet of the Master." Is one right and the other wrong? No. Duty and Devotion are both necessary, but there must be a balance.

Many of you know what entertaining unplanned visitors is like and why Martha is flustered and feeling more and more frustrated with each passing moment. The first part of verse 40 in Luke 10 tells us, *"But Martha was distracted with much serving."* The sense of the word translated "distracted" here is "to be pulled away" or "dragged away." The implication is that Martha wanted to hear Jesus herself; she wanted to be seated at His feet too, but she was pulled away by the sense of her "duties." Fretting about the meal has robbed her of the joy of her service to the Lord, thus the manipulation ensues. We should, of course, take our responsibilities seriously, but not take ourselves so seriously to the point we overestimate our importance. The problem did not lie in the *work* Martha was doing. It was the *attitude* with which she was doing it that became the problem. Martha's problem was one of balance; between the going and doing, and the sitting and listening.

I truly believe Martha wanted to honor Jesus. I even believe she began her work with the right attitude. Many of you can identify with this. You begin the task of a huge festive meal (like Thanksgiving) with the greatest of enthusiasm, but as time passes you come to realize you are running out of time and you cannot possibly finish everything you planned to do before the entire family will show up.

Around our house on Thanksgiving Day, my bride actually begins cooking the day before! It's a big deal. And it smells good! She goes all out in making it a special meal for all of us. While I'm watching the *Thanksgiving Macy Day Parade* she's working hard to ensure that all of us will have wonderful memories of the occasion. And the beautiful thing about her is, she does it with a willing, genuinely loving heart. Sure, the kids and I all pitch in to help, but she's the architect that makes it all happen.

Since our own families live so far away, we usually invite others who are in the same position to celebrate the Thanksgiving meal with us. We bring them in and make them a part of our family for the day. On most occasions they arrive on time and everything is ready. But there have been a few instances when they arrived early! And my bride, in her beautiful, loving way, would welcome them in even though she wasn't ready, and just keep preparing while entertaining and including them too.

For some people, the arrival of early guests when they're not ready can throw off their entire rhythm for the day. It messes everything up and then the emotions begin to swirl. When that happens, they get angry; angry at themselves for letting themselves get in this fix and angry with anyone else who might have made a difference in accomplishing their goals. Martha was like that; the harder she worked the more worked up she became. Some people "burn out" in service, but Martha was "burned up" in hers. It is bad enough to have everything to do. It is even worse when we can think of someone who we do not feel is pulling his or her weight and who has let us down. That is what I see happening to Martha. . .*and the manipulation started*.

In the second part of verse 40 (continuing in Luke 10) Martha finally exploded and she comes boiling out of the kitchen, red-faced, and furious and says; *"Lord, do You not care that my sister has left me to serve alone? Therefore tell her to help me."* She doesn't even call her sister by name. In her defense perhaps she had already done everything she could think of to attract Mary's attention and signal her that she needed help. We all have ways we use to get a message across to manipulate the situation. We clear our throats. We make attention-getting motions and so on. For me, I attempt to give Butch "the eye". Over the years she's very well aware of the "the eye" look. You've got your look or manipulative jester that accompanies your desire. We've all got them.

As you'll read in the text, Martha cannot get Mary's attention. Have you ever noticed how we are even more irritated when the other person ignores us? When Butch ignores "the eye", it drives me crazy!

Have you ever tried to just ignore somebody but you couldn't do it? Reminds me of the conversation between Ned and Phil in the movie GROUNDHOG DAY.

Famous Movie Quote:

1993 Movie GROUNDHOG DAY [3]
Ned: *"Phil? Hey, Phil? Phil! Phil Connors? Phil Connors, I thought that was you!"*
Phil: *"Hi, how you doing? Thanks for watching."*
[Starts to walk away]
Ned: *"Hey, hey! Now, don't you tell me you don't remember me because I sure as heckfire remember you."*
Phil: *"Not a chance."*
Ned: *"Ned. . . Ryerson. "Needlenose Ned"? "Ned the Head"? C'mon, buddy. Case Western High. Ned Ryerson: I did the whistling belly-button trick at the high school talent show? Bing! Ned Ryerson: got the shingles real bad senior year, almost didn't graduate? Bing, again. Ned Ryerson: I dated your sister Mary Pat a couple times until you told me not to anymore? Well?"*
Phil: *"Ned Ryerson?"*
Ned: *"Bing!"*
Phil: *"Bing."*

Mary was willing to face Martha's anger because sitting at the feet of Jesus meant everything to her at this point. Whatever Martha has already done to get Mary's attention, she is totally exasperated now and speaks directly to Jesus. There is an accusation in her voice when she says, *"Lord, do You not care that my sister has left me to serve alone? Therefore tell her to help me."* (Again Luke 10:40)

Martha was angry with Mary for being so selfish and she is angry at Jesus for allowing this to go on. Notice that Martha addressed her irritation to Jesus and in a way trying to manipulate Him into doing something; you have to admit that she is one gutsy woman.

Martha is accusing Jesus of not caring for her because she was sure that if Jesus really cared for her, He would tell Mary to get up and help her. Today she would say something to the effect of, "Lord you know what a ding bat my sister is, but you are a part of the problem too. You tell her to get her sweet self in here and help me!" In saying this, she not only rebuked and attempted to manipulate her sister, but also the One for whom all of these preparations are being made, Jesus.

But then Jesus puts it all into perspective, which He always does, when He responds to Martha in Luke 10:41-42. *"And Jesus answered and said to her, 'Martha, Martha,* (which sounds like Jan Brady when calling on her sister, "Marsha, Marsha, Marsha!") *you are worried and troubled about many things. But one thing is needed, and Mary has chosen that good part, which will not be taken away from her.'"*

The equalizer of all manipulative endeavors, Jesus, had spoken Truth to bring everyone back to reality. Oh that we would learn this same reality in our everyday lives instead of running around trying to manipulate others for our own gain.

Moses, Aaron, and the Golden Calf

Speaking of famous Cecil B. DeMille movies, I can't help but mention his 1956 classic rendition of *"The Ten Commandments"* starring Charlton Heson, Yul Brynner, and Anne Baxter. A great movie to watch, but an even greater story to find a multitude of examples of manipulation that took place during that time. Let's look at one of those examples.

Exodus 32:1-14 tells us a story of manipulation that took place through the man of God, Aaron, the mouthpiece and brother of Moses in a very rapid period of time. Never before had a people been so privileged as Israel. They had just been liberated, set free after 400 years of slavery. Their nation, Israel, was being born, and they were soon going to be given a homeland; they had been chosen by God to be His followers, the people of God! They were to be His witnesses to the other nations of the earth of truth; that there is only one true and living God.

As we read this Old Testament story in Exodus, Moses had ascended Mount Sinai to receive the civil and religious laws of God; the laws that were to form them into a nation and govern them as a people. But abruptly and sadly, a catastrophic tragedy struck all because Moses had been on the mountain too long! In their impatience and forgetfulness, the people turned to Aaron, manipulating him to create other gods in direct violation of the first two commandments: Exodus 20:3, *"You shall have no other gods before me"*, and Exodus 20:4 "You *shall not make for yourself an idol."* The Israelites turned away from God. They lost their faith and trust in Him, and denied, rejected, and rebelled against Him.

Instead of trusting God and waiting upon Him, the people chose to take things into their own hands, do their own thing, manipulate each other as well as Aaron, and go their own way. The end result is a horrific worshipping of the golden calf. We do not know the conversation verbatim that took place between the Israelites and Aaron, but it must have been pretty intense for Aaron to go along with it so quickly!

Does it sound familiar? Can we relate to the people of Israel? How often do we lose our faith and trust in the God who has chosen and delivered us? Instead we choose to take matters into our own hands, do our own thing, manipulate our individual courses, and go our own way? What happens when we do this?

Not only do we break our relationship with God, and miss out on the good plans He has for our lives, but we also fail to live out our calling and Kingdom Assignment, to witness to the world for Christ, who has called, saved, and empowered us.

When the people saw that Moses was so tardy in coming down from the mountain, they gathered around Aaron with an ungodly form of manipulation and control and said, *"Come, make us gods who will go before us. As for this fellow Moses who brought us up out of Egypt, we don't know what has happened to him."* (Exodus 32:1) In other words, they were looking for a quick fix. Something to fill that God-shaped void. Anything would do. So, taking their jewelry, Aaron fashions a golden calf and proclaims it as the object of their worship.

The next day they have a festival, which included making sacrifices before the calf, eating, drinking, and reveling, which means to have a boisterous, wild party. . . an orgy if you will! And we see that this golden calf, this false god, demands nothing from them spiritually or morally. They move back into the realm of darkness and confusion in no time flat after being manipulated by the enemy himself.

It sure can happen fast, can it not? One moment we are being rescued from slavery to sin and death by following the Risen Christ. The next moment we find ourselves, once again, in bondage to the very things that caused us so much pain and confusion in the first place.

You'll remember the response of Moses when he comes down the mountain to find the people of God reveling in sin. He was outraged! He didn't like it at all! He had been with God, and now, to see God's people like this? Some changes were going to be made immediately! Those who truly loved God would need to return to the heart of who they were as a people and to God as their Lord. Moses meant business and began the work at hand to make it right. Oh that we might do the same after manipulation has taken place! To get back to the work at hand, fulfilling the God-given destiny upon our lives, walking out our Kingdom Assignments!

Eve and The Serpent

Probably the best place to examine Satan's tactic and methodology of temptation through manipulation is the temptation of Eve in Genesis 3:1-6 (NIV) *Now the serpent was more cunning than any beast of the field which the LORD God had made. And he said to the woman, "Has God indeed said, 'You shall not eat of every tree of the garden'?" And the woman said to the serpent, "We may eat the fruit*

64

of the trees of the garden; but of the fruit of the tree which is in the midst of the garden, God has said, 'You shall not eat it, nor shall you touch it, lest you die.'" Then the serpent said to the woman, "You will not surely die. For God knows that in the day you eat of it your eyes will be opened, and you will be like God, knowing good and evil." So when the woman saw that the tree was good for food, that it was pleasant to the eyes, and a tree desirable to make one wise, she took of its fruit and ate. She also gave to her husband with her, and he ate.

As you can see, the serpent came to Eve with the full intention of manipulating her to partake of the forbidden fruit. He had a plan conceived within his very being to come against the creation of God, mankind. With evil intentions motivating him, he approached Eve, God's child, and manipulated her. We're not sure when reading the text the amount of time that took place between the temptation and when Eve actually partook, but we do know that no matter how long or short it was, the serpent was successful. He got the ball rolling into (what we now live as a way of life in our world) a life of sin, pain, and heartache.

The fact is the serpent, the devil, will do everything at his disposal to manipulate you to partake of those things in life God never intended for you to have. His whole motivation is nothing but destruction and pain. As long as we buy into his lies and deceptive practices we will never be able to partake of the full blessings of God in our lives.

God has greater things in store for our lives than we can possibly imagine and we're forfeiting those blessings by buying into the manipulative nature of the enemy and our flesh. If we only knew how much greater the impact our lives would have if we were to say "no" to the fleshly desires and temptations of the enemy that are around us. If we could see a glimpse of the supernatural blessings and outpouring of God's presence upon our lives as a result of our obedience to Him, we would be blown away!

I am convinced one of the most effective and powerful ways to overcome deception, manipulation, and the attacks of the enemy is to *have a passion for God's Presence that outweighs our passion for the world.* To be in God's manifest Presence ever so intimately that the world completely pales in comparison to His Glory is when our passion for His Presence comes forth in reality. We will then begin to see the manipulative devices of the enemy for what they are, a pack of lies and deceit. It is when we are *sitting on the lap of Jesus that our eyes are opened to the reality of what He truly has in store for our lives.*

I love the scriptures that encourage us to come into His presence like it's stated in Psalm 95:2 (ESV), "*Let us come into His Presence with thanksgiving; let us make a joyful noise to Him with songs of praise!*" The original translation of the phrase, "*come into His Presence*" is literally to be cheek-to-cheek with God. And the best way I know to be cheek-to-cheek with someone is to be sitting on their lap. Therefore; as we come into His Presence, He is asking us to sit on His lap and be cheek-to-cheek with Him, to become intimate with Him in every area of our lives. It is then that we will find our passion for His Presence outweighing our passion for the world. This passion will give us the unction to come against the manipulative efforts of the devil and of our flesh.

Question: Are you sitting on His lap? Are you cheek-to-cheek with God? If you need some time to reflect on where you are with God, right now would be a good time to do just that. Pause for a few moments right now and reflect.

Now. . . There's more to learn through these Biblical examples of manipulation, so let's move on.

Esau, Son of Isaac and Grandson of Abraham

After twenty years of barrenness suddenly Rebekah becomes pregnant with twins. The children were fraternal twins and we quickly learn that Esau appears to have his mother's aggressive personality, whereas Jacob tends to be like his father. Isaac, the passive Patriarch (who literally did little more than follow in his father's footsteps), prefers his aggressive outgoing son Esau, the son he was unable to be. Rebekah prefers her passive son, perhaps one she can mold (manipulate) into her image of a son. Jacob becomes a homebody. He learns from his mom to deal with the world by means of guile and manipulation. She over-protects her weaker child.

As Esau grew into an outdoorsman and a skilled hunter (not unlike his Uncle Ishmael) he became the embodiment of a masculine man (who goes out to dominate nature) in control. Esau was born with an aggressive personality. Jacob was born as a "mild man of the tents". However, by grasping onto his brother's heel, Jacob invested much of his life striving to be like his aggressive brother. Esau, on the other hand, with his mild personality was content to be as he was created.

Isaac, the passive patriarch, thus gravitates naturally toward Esau and openly displays his preference for him. He finds his aggressive masculine value system attractive and comforting. Isaac can be viewed as the embodiment of passivity, even at critical moments, when his Father Abraham was about to sacrifice him. He recognized Esau's masculine personality and preferred a value system different from his own. Esau is a man's man. How can one imagine life for Esau, the outgoing aggressive personality growing up with an unexciting father? Esau may have been highly active, in all likelihood a 'trouble-maker' as a child, but somehow restrained when with his father.

Isaac loves fresh wild meat; Esau hunts and brings it home, even cooks it for his father. His brother Jacob, whose role is to cook for the family, prefers vegetarian dishes - not what his father desires. One day Esau has a particularly frustrating day hunting. He comes home famished and thirsty, nearly dehydrated, goes to the kitchen and sees Jacob cooking a red lentil dish - hardly to Esau's liking - but he is on the verge of expiration. Jacob, the articulate man of culture makes a trade with his more boorish brother, who has called the lentil soup this "red stuff". Jacob unabashedly formulates and manipulates a deal. The text is clear; Jacob demanded an oath from his brother to sell him the birthright. *'First give me your birthright in exchange'*

(Genesis 25:31). Jacob takes advantage of his weakened brother. Esau, oblivious to anything but his hunger and possible dehydration says, *'Here I am at death's door, what use is a birthright to me?'* (25:32) Esau *'ate, drank, got up and went away'* (25:34), no doubt totally disgusted with his brother.

Jacob, presumably unaware of his mother's divine mission of manipulation, is fearful of his brother but wants to "best" him. Where has Jacob learned this competitive behavior? This issue will come up again when Jacob obtains his father's blessing through covert ways. Jacob had obviously observed and had been trained to manipulate from his mother.

When Isaac *'had grown old'* (27:1) he called Esau and said to him "take your weapons, your quiver and bow; go out into the country and hunt me some game. Make me the kind of appetizing dish I like and bring it to me to eat and I shall bless you from my soul before I die." (27:3-4)

Rebekah overhears Isaac's conversation. She convinces Jacob to deceive and manipulate his father, her husband, the almost blind Patriarch, and to steal the blessing from him. Jacob is fearful of engaging in deceit towards his father, but his mother alleviates his fears by assuming total responsibility for the theft and deception *"On me be the curse, my son, just listen to me."* (27:13). Perhaps Jacob pondered whether a blessing stolen remains a valid blessing.

Rebekah devised a plan of deceit and manipulation to ensure Jacob's receipt of the blessing. She dressed Jacob in Esau's clothing and in the skin of a lamb; Isaac caught the scent and uttered *"Come closer, my son, so I might feel you"* (27:22), which is precisely what Jacob feared.

Did Isaac suspect his wife and younger son might attempt to deceive and manipulate him? When the blind Isaac asked Jacob to identify himself, Jacob responded deceitfully, *"I am Esau your first born . . .* [Isaac responds] Are *you really Esau?"* (27:19). Jacob arrived too quickly from hunting and cooking and Isaac asked, *"How did you succeed so quickly? He said, 'Yahweh made things go well for me"*(27:20). Jacob blatantly lied to his father, manipulating him, using God's name as a witness. His mother engineered the entire plan; she slaughtered and cooked the lamb. It was not God. Isaac senses something is amiss and utters his suspicion, *"The voice is Jacob's voice but the arms are the arms of Esau"* (27:23). Isaac did not trust his ears when he heard the voice of Jacob, nor did he trust his intuition. He could never trust himself after the deception brought on him by his father. The deception is executed, the crime pays, and the theft is successful.

Yet another textbook example of manipulation and abuse.

This next story blows me away

Laban, Rachel, and Leah

You can find this story of manipulation in Genesis 29:16-30. We first meet Leah as a pawn in someone else's manipulative scheme. Jacob was well received by his Uncle Laban and began working for him as a shepherd. After a month, Laban insisted on paying Jacob for his work and even invited him to name his wages. This seemed to be very generous of Laban, but Jacob's uncle was up to no good. Laban knew that Jacob was in love with his daughter, Rachel and wanted to marry her. In that culture, however, you had to pay the bride's father for the privilege of marrying his daughter. Jacob only had his services as a shepherd to offer as payment; so by insisting that Jacob set the bride price, Laban knew he could squeeze more work out of his nephew. Jacob wouldn't want to set the bride price too low lest he insult his future wife. The spirit of manipulation was driving this story down a road of deception and abuse.

In the end, Jacob agreed to work seven years in exchange for Rachel's hand in marriage. Just to put that price into perspective, jewelers today suggest spending two months' salary when buying a wedding ring for the bride. I don't remember spending that much on Butch's ring when we were married in 1980, thanks to a friend who owned a jewelry shop; but all in all, wedding rings can be expensive.

Although Jacob had agreed to pay an exorbitant price for Rachel, he didn't mind. We're told that the seven years seemed like a few days since Jacob was so in love. The long awaited wedding, however, ended in disaster. After the vows were exchanged and the marriage consummated, Jacob discovered he had married Leah, Rachel's older sister! How could something like that happen? Crafty ol' Uncle Laban was behind it all. It wasn't difficult for Laban to pull off the switch since brides in those days wore veils, as is still the case in many

Middle Eastern countries today. But what was Laban's motive? It was simple; he wanted to extort another seven years of work out of Jacob in return for Rachel's hand in marriage; and thus, he manipulated the situation to make it happen.

In Laban, Jacob had met his match. The deceiver was now the one deceived. The manipulator had become the manipulated. Jacob now understood what his father Isaac must have felt like when he had tricked him into thinking he was blessing Esau. It is perhaps for that reason that Jacob agrees, without much arguing, to work for Laban for another seven years to marry Rachel. That's the part that blows me away! Wow, this guy really loved that girl and wanted to be with her big time!

Isn't it amazing what some people will do and the extreme measures they will take to get what they want? I'm always amazed at the degree of deception and manipulation we will go to in order to fulfill the fleshly desires of their hearts. It seems there is no remorse or care that they hurt the people around them just so they can be comfortable and that his or her particular needs will be met. This is truly a sad story of abuse and manipulation.

Okay. The stories have been told. Now what?

So stories of manipulation occurred in the Bible and we're still doing it today. We seem to have adopted the practices of manipulation right into our modern Church mindsets. The issue of control is something we have to deal with. But, God wants us to be under the control of only one Spirit, - the Holy Spirit as in Romans 8:12-16 (NKJV), *"Therefore, brethren, we are debtors—not to the flesh, to live according to the flesh. For if you live according to the flesh you will die; but if by the Spirit you put to death the deeds of the body, you will live. For as many as are led by the Spirit of God, these are sons of God. For you did not receive the spirit of bondage again to fear, but you received the Spirit of adoption by whom we cry out, 'Abba, Father.' The Spirit Himself bears witness with our spirit that we are children of God."*

In Galatians 5:22-25 (NKJV) it is written, *"But the fruit of the Spirit is love, joy, peace, longsuffering, kindness, goodness, faithfulness, gentleness, self-control. Against such there is no law. And those who are Christ's have crucified the flesh with its passions and desires. If we live in the Spirit, let us also walk in the Spirit."*

The Holy Spirit has set us free to live for righteousness and to no longer be under sin's rule. When we yield to someone with a controlling spirit, when we as the Church allow ourselves to be manipulated, our freedom in the Holy Spirit is hindered because we're following another spirit's will. This can have disastrous effects, especially in a Church body, religious institution, or small group ministry. It can unleash strife and cause the presence and anointing of God to lift from a ministry. Since the controlling spirit is only placated when it is yielded to, the leaders must be ready to resist and rebuke the controlling person in love, which we'll look at later.

Both in Biblical times and in the "here and now," the abuse of power involves a harmful and destructive pattern of leadership

73

that diverts organizational power for personal use at the expense of others. Abuse of power thrives in a culture of fear! Leaders are afraid of losing their power - subordinates are afraid of confronting leadership, knowing how dangerous the pathway is for those who take that road. Loyalty is emphasized in such an environment in order to distract a person from the things that are really occurring. An individual's loyalty is placed into question when leadership is challenged. Mutual intimidation lies just beneath the surface of what seems safe to talk about or to question!

Oh the tangled web we weave.

Time to Get Real. . .

1. Romans 8:12-16 cautions us to not live according to the flesh, but rather according to the Spirit. What are the benefits or consequences of your choice?
2. Abuse of power thrives in a culture of _____.
3. Why do you think God blessed some of those characters in the Bible even though they obviously manipulated others?
4. With manipulation, do you think the end justifies the means?
5. What can you learn from these characters in what NOT to do in your life?
6. When we manipulate others, how does that affect our walk with Christ?

7. Why might a controlling spirit cause the presence or anointing of God to lift away?

8. Have you ever experienced this form of manipulation? What did you do about it?

Chapter 4

"What's the Harm?"

"What's the Harm?"

So what's the harm with a little manipulation taking place in the Church? As we've seen, manipulation is found all throughout the Bible in the lives of people, and they seemed to survive through it. Sure, they had to pay a price for their ways and some of them paid the price of death; but all in all, the manipulation continued. So, what is the big deal if we deceive others and manipulate them? After all, we live in a society where manipulation is pretty much accepted as a way of life. As the old saying goes, "Everyone is doing it." And everyone seems to be doing "it" within the Church too!

Yes, everyone is doing it; but the Truth remains that we, as the Church, are not supposed to be like the world. 1 John 2:15-17 (NKJV) makes this very clear. *Do not love the world or the things in the world. If anyone loves the world, the love of the Father is not in him. For all that is in the world—the lust of the flesh, the lust of the eyes, and the pride of life—is not of the Father but is of the world.*

And the world is passing away, and the lust of it; but he who does the will of God abides forever.

I like what it says in John 15:19 (NLT). *The world would love you as one of its own if you belonged to it, but you are no longer part of the world. I chose you to come out of the world, so it hates you.*

With all of that being said and with all of the scriptures given to us in God's Word instructing us to be separate from the world, we still haven't figured it out. We seem to go about our lives with this thought it is okay to dabble in sin. We seem to go about our lives with the mindset that what happens in our Churches, the abusive and manipulative actions of people, is okay. Why, it's been happening for a long time and nothing is going to stop it. So, who cares?

Well, I care and let me tell you why. Let me show you one of the main reasons why this attitude of manipulating the Church must stop.

I am increasingly concerned at how frequently I meet people that have become "detached" from the Church. The term for them is called, "de-churched Christians", those that have simply dropped-out of Church. They want nothing to do with the organized system of "church-going. They have distanced themselves from being a part of any type of fellowship and they refuse to come together with other Christians on a regular basis under the roof of the "church". I have discovered there really is such a thing as "de-churched Christians." That phrase is not an oxymoron. There really are spiritually battered Christians who do not go to church and who have no intention of doing so. They are usually former Church members who can readily cite long lists of grievances.

Here are four case studies that I recently read from Jim Miller in his writing, *"Recognizing and Recovering from Spiritual Abuse."* [1]

Case #1: Fund Raising

Theresa and Bob, both active Church members, left their Church because they felt too much pressure was put on them to contribute to yet another "unneeded" building project. Receiving offerings, they claimed, consumed too much of both the Sunday worship service and their limited income. Already financially taxed beyond their budget, the strain was becoming oppressive. They questioned the wisdom of launching yet another expansion program and were bluntly informed by their pastor the building project was, in fact, "ordained by God." The couple was sternly warned their criticism was "subversive" and to "stop causing trouble." This reprimand was followed by a series of Sunday sermons underscoring members' spiritual duty of submission to their leaders' authority. Theresa and Bob left the Church more than a year ago and have yet to join another Church. Theresa claims she now feels "closer to the Lord" since leaving the Church than she did while there and that she no longer suffers from chronic depression.

Case #2: Volunteer over Marriage

George was working 48 hours a week on his job and volunteering another 25 at the church. A talented musician, he was recruited by the Church orchestra. He was also asked to join the baseball team, the parish committee and the board. In time, his marriage suffered and eventually his wife left. George was too late. He tried to free up his day-planner by resigning from some of the Church positions he held but was informed by the pastor that he was "needed." He was assured that if he put the "kingdom" first, God would restore his home. Frustrated and fatigued, George eventually dropped out of Church altogether. Too late! His mortally wounded marriage died. Today, George is a bitter man and vows never to return to Church.

Case #3: Professional Ministry Not Enough

Mark, an active Church member of a thriving Charismatic church and a bright medical intern, was required to work long hours through the week, including many Sundays. This professional constraint interfered with his volunteer duties at the church. The pastor, expressing concern for Mark's "spiritual development," brazenly suggested he seek a career change. Mark explained that medicine was his lifelong chosen career and his internship was temporary. Anyhow, he added, wasn't his particular career a ministry in itself? The pastor remained uncompromising in his demands and there was no further discussion. Thinking the disagreement was resolved, Mark was humiliated the following Sunday by a public "prophetic word" from a staff member. Of course, the associate affirmed the pastor's mandate, even predicting dreadful consequences if the "prophecy" was not obeyed. Mark prayed but remained solid in his decision. Within weeks, the young intern was summarily discharged from his duties in the Church and his membership placed on "inactive" status. Hurt and angered, Mark left the Church. Today, he is a successful M.D. with a flourishing practice, but he has not returned to Church.

Case #4: Political Agenda

Robert and Glenda, alarmed that their Church was becoming preoccupied with a "right-wing political agenda," approached their pastor with their concerns. The meeting went badly. Threatened by their perceived insubordination, the pastor accused them of being "unsubmissive to spiritual authority," and warned them of falling prey to a defiant "spirit of Korah." During the following weeks, the couple suspected the leadership of the Church was ostracizing them and they were inexplicably removed from the Church mailing list and prayer chain. They eventually took the hint, stopped attending Church and joined the swelling ranks of de-churched Christians.

So, here's the harm. . .

Yes, manipulation is taking place, and yes people have become immune to it for the most part. They just sit in their places of worship week after week, enduring the abuse. Most of them are not even aware it's taking place. It has become a part of who they are; they don't even realize they are in bondage and that they are being kept from flying to the degree God has called them to fly. They think they are flying, but in reality they are plummeting beneath the clouds of true freedom.

But then there are those who have come to the knowledge and awareness of the manipulation and abuse. Whether it is disguised as meek and innocent or is flagrantly in your face, they refuse to be a part of it. And with that awareness comes the decision to leave the Church. I don't blame them. No one should have to sit under the abusive hand of a leader who is controlling them and keeping them from being all that God has called them to be.

How sad it is that many people become disenfranchised with the whole idea of the Church. They see the abuse that takes place and want nothing to do with it. Many of them leave, never to return again. Don't get me wrong; I know you don't have to go to church to be a Christian. I'm aware of the fact there are tons of people sitting in our churches today that aren't even close to being Christians, a true follower of Christ. Going to church will never get you into heaven. But being a part of THE CHURCH, the body of Christ, is the most important aspect of life itself! Having a relationship with Jesus Christ and being a part of His family, the Church, is what it's all about!

Some people leave the church building and leave the Church body at the same time - never to return to the family of God. There have been untold souls that have walked away from God simply because they want nothing to do with the modern day Church world and the practices that take place on a regular basis. They get enough abuse at work and home - why should they come to church and get spiritually abused as well? So, they leave church and Church all together. That, my friends, is just one of the reasons why manipulation is a big deal. When just one soul walks away from God, the heart of God is painfully saddened. He is not willing that any should perish, but desires ALL might come to Him and have everlasting life!

The old Church mindsets must change if we're going to make an impact for the Kingdom of God.

Manipulation in the Church – it's a big deal!

Time to Get Real. . .

1. 1 John 2:15-17 tells us not to love the world or what's in it. What three things are in the world?

2. What does God's love look like according to 1 Corinthians 13? Do you feel Church leadership has lost that kind of love?

3. How many people do you know that used to attend Church on a regular basis but have quit due to being spiritually abused by someone within the Church leadership? How did that affect you when they left? Was there a part of you that thought those people were just being a bit "over sensitive?"

4. Have you ever passed judgment upon them as being those who just couldn't submit to authority?

5. Who do you know that has turned their back on God as a result of a bad experience in the Church?

6. Do you think it's a problem in the modern day culture of the Church world or are they just isolated cases that involve isolated people who are abused and leaving their places of worship?

Chapter 5

"Church Mindsets vs. Kingdom Mindsets"

"Church Mindsets vs. Kingdom Mindsets"

*W*hat do I mean by "mindsets"? A mindset describes an attitude, outlook, approach, belief, or conviction regarding a matter. According to the Encarta English Dictionary, it is "a set of beliefs or a way of thinking that determine somebody's behavior and outlook".

It is my opinion that one of the problems within the Church body today is the mindset we have of seeing through the lens of each of our own experiences. There are many contributing factors that lead us to spiritually manipulate others and allow ourselves to be spiritually manipulated. One of the areas I want to explore in more detail is the area of having a Kingdom-of-God mindset as opposed to an old, traditional Church mindset. As you will see, they should be the same, but they are not. It is the plan of God that the Church has a Kingdom of God mindset, but we have distorted that truth over the years. We have relied upon tradition as opposed to the fresh newness of the Spirit of God.

I have found that those with true Kingdom mindsets are much less likely to abuse and manipulate others as opposed to those with the traditional Church mindset.

Let me explain

As I wrote in the beginning of this book, we cannot go to "Church." It's impossible to *go* to something that you *are*. The fact is, we don't *go* to church to worship God; we come together as The Church (the Body of Christ) to celebrate Him. In the American mindset, which is very often the worldly mindset of the Church, there is a vast difference as to what the Church is really all about.

If we want to make an impact for the Kingdom of God, investing in the Kingdom, then we must be Kingdom-minded people and not church-minded people. Author Joseph Mattera [1] has written some great articles on this subject that I'll blend in with my own teaching as well as other teachings throughout this chapter. It is my great hope you will desire to be a Kingdom-Minded person, carrying out the Will of God in your life – Investing in the Kingdom without manipulating others to get this accomplished!

Okay, get on with it already

Okay, I will. As we begin this subject of the difference between the two mindsets, keep in mind what Jesus, John the Baptist, and the apostles went about proclaiming. We find them proclaiming the Kingdom–not the Church. Matthew 3:2 (NLT) *Repent of your sins and turn to God, for the Kingdom of Heaven is near.*

Matthew 4:17 (NKJV) *From that time Jesus began to preach and to say, "Repent, for the Kingdom of Heaven is at hand."*

Matthew 10:7 (NKJV) *And as you go, preach, saying, "The Kingdom of heaven is at hand."*

Acts 28:30-31 (NKJV) *Then Paul dwelt two whole years in his own rented house, and received all who came to him, preaching the Kingdom of God and teaching the things which concern the Lord Jesus Christ with all confidence, no one forbidding him.*

Although the Church is in the Kingdom, it is not the entire Kingdom

"Kingdom" denotes the rule of God over the whole cosmos, not just a single entity on the earth, like the Church. In spite of this, some preaching today strongly encourages people to make a weekly two-hour commitment to come to a building on Sundays or Saturdays and to give tithes to support that building! This is because a Spirit of Religion has captivated the Church (which we'll look at in the next chapter) and blinded the minds of Church leaders, so we now have a very limiting Church mindset instead of a Kingdom perspective. The negative results of this cannot be overstated. As I said earlier, you cannot *go* to something that you *are* – thus we must come to the realization of what we really are as a Kingdom person. What will follow will be a decreased measure of manipulation within the Church Body.

In essence. . .

- Those with a **Kingdom mindset** regard Christianity as a Biblical world/life view centered on the person of Jesus Christ who is Lord and King of all creation. This has vast political, economic, and sociological implications.
- Those with a traditional **Church mindset** view Jesus merely as the King of the Church, not the King of all earthly secular kings.

Matthew 15:3 Jesus says, *"Why do you yourselves transgress the commandment of God for the sake of your tradition?"*

I like what Frank Viola says, "History is repeating itself today. Contemporary Christianity has fallen into the errors of both the Pharisees and the Sadducees."[2] Sadly, this seems to be an accurate description of the direction many in the Church are heading today.

We have limited the impact of the Church Body to a set of rules, regulations, traditions, and manipulation.

The following are 16 contrasts between these two mindsets to give you a clearer picture of what I'm talking about. Feel free to scan your own life to see if any of these comparisons ring true in your spirit. Identifying the difference between the two will be a great asset in your ability to challenge the attitudes and actions of those who try to manipulate their own personal agendas.

Contrasting a Kingdom Mindset with a Church Mindset

1. CALLINGS

A Kingdom mindset releases people to their vocational callings in the marketplace. A Church mindset controls people by marginalizing their marketplace callings and emphasizing only their Sunday ministries.

To put it simply, a Kingdom mindset trains people for all of life. A traditional Church mindset trains people only for church life. We have the opinion in today's viewpoint of the church that it's about "training for reigning within the walls of the church." The Kingdom mindset has the viewpoint that the Church is "training for reigning outside the walls of the church."

Many of our modern day Bible Colleges, Universities and Seminaries have the viewpoint of training students to become "pastors, teachers, evangelists, etc. all within the walls of the church setting" as opposed to outside of the walls. It is sadly in these places of learning we have taught our ministers and Church leaders how to manipulate others to make this happen. Though it is not necessarily an intended philosophy of "evil" or spiritual abuse, it is beneath the surface of what takes place in the environments of the classroom and campus living.

If we're not living our lives for God, training and discipling people to make an impact in every aspect of their lives, then we're not living with a Kingdom mindset.

A true Kingdom-minded Church equips 100% of the saints to minister in all things in every realm of life. Those with an old Church mindset have, as their primary goal a desire to equip 2-3% of the congregation who are called to be full-time Church pastors, ministers, and missionaries - thus manipulating people to become a part of an elite group of saints "called by God." Are we not ALL "called by God" in every walk of life?

A Kingdom mindset releases all saints as ministers in the marketplace. A Church mindset merely trains people to serve in a church building on Sundays. It's all so very backwards.

The Sunday or Saturday services are important; but when we limit ourselves to only those times, we are completely limiting the role of the body of Christ. What I teach our people at Eastgate Community Church is that we come together as the Church on Sundays to celebrate Jesus Christ. The rest of the week, the other six days, we're in the marketplace of life - *Being* the Church;

carrying out our Kingdom assignments given to us by God. Wherever you work, that's your Kingdom assignment. Wherever you go to school, that's your Kingdom assignment. Wherever you live, that's your Kingdom assignment. Wherever you play, that's your Kingdom assignment.

Church is not to be relegated to a Sunday morning existence, while we go about "real life" the rest of the week. Church is supposed to be happening 24-7. That's Kingdom. Your ministry is in the marketplace of your life as well as in the church building! So don't allow those who are speaking into your life spiritually lead you to believe any other way. It's manipulation.

Let's look at the second contrast between a Kingdom mindset and Church mindset.

2. MONEY

A Kingdom mindset creates wealth to transform a community and nation. A Church mindset motivates giving to build our own church programs and buildings.

Basically, the Kingdom mindset is external, while the traditional Church mindset is internal. Most Churches in today's culture focus more on what is happening with our programs and ministries, as opposed to what is happening in the culture around us in our communities.

That is why 1/3 of our vision at Eastgate is to SERVE. Serving our community – working to create wealth for the Kingdom of

God to transform our communities and nation around us. What we do at Eastgate is not about Eastgate Community Church – it's about our community, state, nation, and around the world!

Money; what a driving force in our world today. Sadly, the Church often holds the opinion that raising money is about them and their "thing", as opposed to being God's "thing" which translates to souls. How many times have we been encouraged to give of our finances so we can just build a building or fund another project, as opposed to giving of our finances to help further the Kingdom of God? How many times have you felt manipulated to give of your finances for the sake of the church building?

One of the aspects of Eastgate I loved during the first 6 years of our existence as a Church was not having our own building in which to worship. For 6 years every Sunday we set up our equipment in a rented building and tore it back down again. Yes, it would have been wonderful to have had our own building right from the beginning so we didn't have to set up and tear down our "stuff" every Sunday when we came together to celebrate! It would have been wonderful not to have to ask the wonderful volunteers to be there early to set up and stay late to tear down week after week. That would have been great. And I know that those tireless servants would have been thankful as well. Though they never complained about it, I know it took its toll on them to make that sacrifice.

But as much as I would have loved to have had our own building, I think it was a blessing for us NOT to – for I believe it taught us

93

right from the beginning the fact that we're not supposed to be about building buildings – but building The Church! It instilled the reality in each of us that the Church is the Body, not the building. We're not about brick and mortar; we're all about souls!

Stop Riding Dead Horses

3. DEAD HORSES

A Kingdom mindset will have a funeral for a dead horse. A Church mindset will keep riding the dead horse.

If a program is dead in a church. . .then it needs a funeral, and the people need to move on. Investing time, energy, and money into something that is dead will not revive it. Celebrate the fact that "that" program had its day. . . and then move on.

If the horse is dead – get off it and have a funeral. Too many people with the traditional Church mindset keep riding that dead horse; why it's tradition to do so, right? Too many leaders in the Church are trying to keep their favorite horse running by manipulating the people "under them" to keep it going so that they'll look good. I've experienced this myself first hand. I can remember having a ministry in our Church that I thought was the next best thing since sliced bread, and I did everything I could to prop that ministry up and to keep the attention of the people on that horse. After all, the horse was winning when it first came out of the gate, so why shouldn't it keep winning? And, it made me look good in the process!

The problem with a dead horse is that it's dead and not going to take you anywhere. No matter how hard you kick, how much food you give it, how much tender loving care you apply to it, it's still dead. As well, you really look dumb riding it! The world looks at what you're riding and they want nothing to do with it! It's dead. Churches, Christian organizations, and religious institutions look silly as they ride those dead horses; no wonder the world wants nothing to do with the Church world.

An old Church mindset will attempt to manufacture energy towards something just because they want it to happen and will manipulate others in very "holy" ways to get them to keep it going. "We've always done it that way and we think we should continue to do it that way. The traditions must continue!" A Kingdom mindset will realize when that particular ministry, tradition or idea has run its course, let it die, and move on.

What's Number Four?

Thanks for asking.

4. RELIGION

A Kingdom mindset is willing to go against the norms of religion. A Church mindset plays it safe and goes with the flow.

Jesus was one who went against the norms of religion in His day. He was a renegade. I believe that Christianity over the past two thousand years has moved from a tribe of renegades to a religion of conformists and often we manipulate others to keep it that way.

My friend Steve Kline recently wrote this. . .

"I think it is hard for today's Christian to understand just what a radical, non-conformist Jesus was. No one understood what Jesus was talking about during His earthly ministry. Even the apostles needed the parables explained. People couldn't understand Him because His thinking was so counter to the current way of thinking. But, for today's Christians we are so familiar with the gospels, Jesus' parables, and the meaning of the parables that we can't understand why it was so hard for those around Jesus to understand what He was talking about. But, Jesus was talking Kingdom while the Pharisees and other Jews were talking church (or synagogue or political Messiah or whatever you want to call it). We don't appreciate how radical Jesus' thinking was when compared to the thinking of the world. We soooo water down those red letters in the Bible because no one could really live like that today, that was only for Jesus' time, my situation is different, etc. Jesus even gives examples (divorce) of how the kingdom was watered down by the Jews.

96

The Church is seeking change in the culture by adjusting behaviors (don't do this, don't do that, do this, do that) – both of those in the church and of those not in the church. But, the culture is merely a reflection of current thinking. If we want a kingdom culture, then we need to adopt kingdom thinking. Then the behaviors will take care of themselves. It is what comes out of the heart that makes us impure.

What is the standard? Will it be kingdom thinking – no holds barred? Or, will we say that's too hard and go for something less, but something that we rationalize is better than the thinking of the world so that makes it good?"

There will be spiritual leaders in your life who enjoy the status quo, satisfied and content with where you are and where the Church is. There will be those who will do everything they can to keep things as they are and manipulate you in ways to keep it that way. It may have even been said that, "Thus saith the Lord. . ." For too long, many in spiritual authority have played the "God told me" card to get what they've wanted. Once that card is played, you cannot unplay it. You're stuck. And the fact is, either it WAS God who spoke or it WASN'T! Time will usually tell.

Use discernment Church! It was never God's plan for us to be content and satisfied with where we are. It was never His plan for us to just sit back and enjoy the comforts of life while the rest of the world around us made its way to hell. **We've got to stand up, speak up, and be the Church, expecting more in every area of our lives!**

Remember this in Ephesians 3:20 (NKJV). *Now to Him who is able to do exceedingly abundantly above all that we ask or think, according to the power that works in us!*

Don't allow spiritual manipulators to keep you from having a dream that is bigger than you are. And by all means, begin to carry out that dream! You are the Body of Christ! You are His Bride! So dream big! Get out of your comfortable box and dream! If you've been asked to put your dream on hold, don't do it. God would never ask you to put your dream aside. For Pete's sake, He's the one who gave you the dream in the first place; right? So if He gave you the dream, why would He ask you to put it on hold?!

Keep in mind that timing is everything with God. He is in charge of the timing. He is in charge of fulfilling the dream He has given you. He is responsible for carrying the dream out. You are responsible to keep dreaming!

Mr. Strickland tried to tell McFly he didn't have a chance in the movie BACK TO THE FUTURE. But McFly knew his destiny! He wasn't afraid of his future destiny and didn't allow his past to keep him from dreaming.

Famous Movie Quote:

1985 Movie BACK TO THE FUTURE [3]

Mr. Strickland: *"I noticed your band is on the roster for the dance auditions after school today. Why even bother, McFly? You don't have a chance. You're too much like your old man. No McFly ever amounted to anything in the history of Hill Valley!"*

Marty McFly: *"Yeah, well, history is gonna change."*

Keep in mind that timing is everything with God. He is in charge of the timing. He is in charge of fulfilling the dream that He has given you. He is responsible for carrying the dream out. You are responsible to keep dreaming!

5. POLITICS

A Kingdom mindset has a Biblical approach that integrates the gospel with politics, economics, and public policy. A Church mindset insulates the gospel from politics and public policy.

Have you ever felt like someone in some type of spiritual authority in your life was telling you who you should be and what you should stand for politically? Here in America, have you ever gotten the feeling that if you are a Christian, then you must be a Republican; and if you're not, then you're probably a sin-filled Democrat? For too long we've been manipulated into thinking this stereotype must be right. Well here's the deal. . .

It's a Lie and it's Wrong!

Just because you are a Republican doesn't make you a Christian, and just because you are a Democrat doesn't make you a Christian. And it goes without saying that just because you are a Republican doesn't make you a sinner even as being a Democrat doesn't make you a sinner. What makes you a Christian is your personal relationship with Christ, regardless of your political views on life! What makes you a sinner is not having relationship with Christ knowing that your sins have been forgiven!

Arrrggghhhhh. Stop being manipulated into thinking you can't have a voice in the political system of the world today! **You are the Church. Speak up!** Know what you stand for as supported through God's Word; don't allow yourself to be manipulated to keep it quiet and shout it to the world of your choosing!

I believe we as The Church, the body of Christ, need to take every aspect of the gospel with us wherever we go. They say there must be a separation between the government and religion, church and state. I say, we need to have such a Kingdom influence in the realm of politics, economics, and public policy that we're making a True difference; an impact for the Kingdom of God in the world in which we daily live!

We shouldn't be insulating ourselves from the politics of the world, but making an impact within the politics of the world! Godly politics should trump the world's system of politics every time. And if anyone tells you otherwise, you're being manipulated. Do not allow your hands to be tied or your mouth to be gagged by those who would try to keep you from speaking and living the Truth of God's Word in the world today.

Let's look at the sixth contrast between a Kingdom mindset and Church mindset.

Manipulators usually have their heads in the clouds

6. HEAD IN THE CLOUDS

A Kingdom mindset has the attitude and heart of pure, humble, weak, empty vessels saved by the grace of God Almighty, walking with Divine authority to serve others. A Church mindset has the attitude that we are the high and mighty ones called by God for such a time as this, to be served, separated and set apart from the world until He calls us home.

Yes, we are supposed to be apart from the world, but we still live in this world. We do not have to live our lives as the world does. We often times separate ourselves from the world in which we live with our head in the clouds of eternity, making no impact for the Kingdom of God whatsoever!

I've heard the phrase used before that some Christians are *"so heavenly minded they are of no earthly good."* Basically, they've got their head in the clouds and only focused on themselves and getting into heaven; and sadly the world around them is falling apart. Society is falling apart, but they're going to heaven and they don't really care about their society.

Friend, the issue is not if you're going to heaven or not! If you've accepted Christ into your heart as John 3:16 declares, you're going to heaven! The true issue is **how many people are you going to take with you?**

When you decide to whom you are going to submit yourself as a spiritual accountability covering, make sure that person is one who understands the difference between having a heart of pure humility and a desire *to* serve, as opposed to those who desire to *be* served. Those that have the mindset of *being served* will manipulate you. Those who have a Kingdom mindset *to serve* others will be those from whom you will receive good Godly teachings and counsel. They will not lead you astray.

Don't forget Romans 12:2. *Do not conform any longer to the pattern of this world, but be transformed by the renewing of your mind. Then you will be able to test and approve what God's will is — His good, pleasing and perfect will.*

The Bible gives us a clear choice here. We can continue to conform to the pattern of this world – in other words we can carry on thinking in the same way as everyone else around us, like we've always thought in the past – or we can decide to think God's way and begin to live in and experience the power of His Kingdom right now. This is what it means to "test and approve God's will"

– the Kingdom of God is simply God's will done here on earth as it is in heaven.

7. THE BIBLE

A Kingdom mindset views the Bible as a blueprint to affect every aspect of society. A Church mindset views the Bible merely as a pietistic (exaggerated, smug, hypocritical attitude) book that enables us to escape the world, enter heaven, and be spiritual.

Kingdom people view God's Word as the blueprint for every aspect of society. They live it, breathe it, and walk it out daily. The Bible is not an escape plan from earth to heaven, but a guide to impact earth so that all might enter into heaven.

I have found the typical person with a traditional Church mindset hardly reads their Bible at all. When they do, it's more likely, they are reading as an assignment or they are at a place in their lives when they are desperate. A Kingdom minded person will read their Bible simply out of their love for God. They will apply it to their lives, make life changes when needed, memorize it, live it, and love it.

At the same time, those who manipulate and abuse others often have knowledge of the Word of God but use it for their own gain. They will find a text out of the Bible that will support their viewpoints as opposed to getting a message from God with a text that will support His viewpoints. I've even known Christians who will attempt to use scripture as a weapon against other Christians in the hope of manipulating and coming against them. They think they look good on the surface because they are quoting scripture, but eventually, the truth of what they are attempting to do will be made known.

The moment we take scripture out of context or use it to try to manipulate someone for our gain, we need to know there will be a day of reckoning. There will be a time when God will no longer allow it to happen. You can't get away with it forever.

God's Idea of Discipleship is Life - on - Life

8. LIFE ON LIFE

A Kingdom mindset believes discipleship is an undeniable reality. A Church mindset believes discipleship is a great idea.

We talk it like crazy, that we must be making disciples. We know it is the Great Commission and God has commanded us to do it. We believe that it must be done and that we will do whatever it takes to make disciples for Christ – but do we? For the most part, we don't. Ask any Church out there today what their weakest link is in their Church body and they will most likely tell you discipleship. It is the greatest need we have at Eastgate Community Church. It is what we are lacking the most. Discipleship is the key to a healthy body!

We have got to stop talking about it and start doing it. It must become THE priority of what we do as a Church body along with the Great Commandment to love God and others. It must become something where we invest our time, talents and money. It must become a part of our DNA, of what we do, and of what we desire. Discipleship!

Spiritual leaders who downplay discipleship or go about it any other way than what God's Word teaches, are manipulating their own agendas outside of God's plan. If their idea of discipleship makes them look good but is completely ineffective for the Kingdom of God, then it is not God's idea of true discipleship. God's idea of discipleship is basically this: life on life. It's when your path of life comes alongside another's path of life and the two of you walk life together; planting the Truths of God's story in His Word so that it brings life and health into every aspect of your respective journeys.

9. TOTAL EMBRACE

In a Kingdom mindset, saints will embrace and love their surrounding unchurched communities. In a Church mindset, saints only embrace converted individuals within their faith communities.

For too long now the Church has expected the unchurched to come to them. We invite the sinners to come to our programs, our services, and to "our thing". We expect them to come at Easter and Christmas, and then they'll get saved. Traditional Church mindset leaders will manipulate in every way possible to get the world to come to them. Leaders will come up with all types of gimmicks and worldly ideas of bringing them in for the sake of growing their Church population, thus making *them* look good. Sure they might look successful in the eyes of the world and in the eyes of their own egotistical hearts, but what about making God look good? This type of thinking is nothing but ungodly manipulation and must come to an end.

Kingdom people don't wait for them to come to us; we go to them! We embrace them out there in their world, in their facet of life, on their turf, in their time – with a heart of love and servant-hood. Our job is not to get them to come to our church on Sundays, but it should be to get them to become a part of the Family of God! In my heart, I could actually care less if people come to Eastgate Community Church. I'm not about building our "Church". My heart is to build the Kingdom of God, His Church! I want them to come to Christ. If they come to Eastgate – so be it; we will welcome them with open arms! But if they go to another location and worship with the family of God there instead, that's quite fine! Kingdom people think about this area of their lives with the bigger picture at hand and will not use manipulation as a form of building their own personal kingdoms.

10. ALTAR CALLS

A Kingdom mindset believes that a person can come to Christ at any time, at any place, with no rigmarole involved. A Church mindset believes salvation only happens at the Altar of the church.

Have you ever attended a worship service or church gathering and listened to someone give an altar call for salvation at the end of a message? I'm sure you've probably heard this hundreds of times in the course of your walk with God. And with that being said, I'm sure you have heard everything in the book in their attempts to get people to the altar. Pushing, pulling, yelling, smiling, crying, pleading, arguing, wrestling, silent treatment or whatever type of manipulation they can come up with to get them there. I've heard it all. I've even used many of these tactics myself. (Okay, not the wrestling one.)

This is one of those Arrrggghhhhh moments for me. Now don't get me wrong, I believe in altar calls and giving people an opportunity to respond to a message. I am a product of an altar call given when I was nine years of age in the small Indian Reservation Church, Harrah Assembly of God, where I grew up. I came down to the altar one Wednesday night and gave my heart to God after my pastor gave an altar call. I believe in altar calls; we have them during our Celebration services at Eastgate and will continue to have them from week to week as the Holy Spirit leads us.

But here's the problem. . .

There are many people with "religious" attitudes that think the only time a person can get "saved" (come to Jesus Christ) is at the altar of a church building after the call has been given by the pastor to come forward. We've accepted the mindset that it is the only way a person can really be repentant. Actually, altar calls for salvation didn't even start until the 1820's and 30's with Charles Finney. Later it was popularized by the Billy Graham crusades when thousands of people would come forward. I praise God for those times. In fact, I was in many of those services myself and saw them come forward. The sad part now, is there are many Church-minded people that still think that's the only way to come to Christ; which it is not. People can come to Christ at any time! Even out there in the world as the Church leads them to Him, wherever they might be spiritually.

Did you know that today there are more people coming to Christ outside the four walls of a church building than there are within the four walls of the church building? The cold reality of it is there are more people who do not have a relationship with Christ outside the walls of our buildings than those inside the buildings! The lost multitudes are not sitting within the walls of our church buildings; they are out there! Kingdom-mindset people take it upon themselves to win them over to Christ *out there*; **not depending upon the pastor to do everything for them during the service.**

There is a trap I've experienced in my ministry when giving an altar call for salvation or any other type of call that I'm sure many others have faced as well. The trap is, we want to look good in what we do as preachers; and if people respond to our messages by coming forward, then the message must have been good. We fall into the mindset that if souls are filling the altars, then people in our congregations will consider us successful at what we do. It's a trap and leads us to manipulate people to respond by coming forward. Kingdom-mindset people take it upon themselves to win them to Christ wherever they are!

My First Altar Call

The first altar call for salvation I gave was at Northwest Bible College in Kirkland, Washington. My bride and I graduated from there. I even proposed to my beautiful bride one enchanting misty evening by Lake Washington at Northwest University (its present name).

As a freshman student I was blessed to travel and sing with a musical ensemble called "The Maranatha Sounds." I was with Maranatha for five years, singing, playing the saxophone, and speaking. We traveled the western side of the United States singing and promoting the college. It was during one of our concerts held at the campus itself I gave this altar call. The then-president of the college, President D.V. Hurst, asked me personally to give the altar call for salvation after the concert at the school's Campus Days. This was the weekend hundreds of new students would be there, as well as potential students who were contemplating making Northwest Bible College their home for the next four years. It was a big deal to be asked to give this altar call. The pressure was on - and I felt it. My peers would be watching, my teachers would be watching, and President Hurst would be watching. I desperately didn't want to let him down. It was an honor to be asked to do this that night and I wanted him to be pleased that he asked me to minister in this way.

We sang our usual set of tunes and then it came to the end of the concert. I stood before the packed chapel and gave the altar call for salvation. I spoke from my heart and gave the message as simply as I could. To my delight, hundreds responded that night for salvation. They flooded the altar! Tears were flowing from those who came forward, as well as my own. The manifest presence of God was in the house! My heart and spirit rang out with joy and thankfulness to the Lord!

That night, God looked good.
But the problem was, I *thought* I looked good too.

The very next weekend, we were traveling as a group to another city to do another concert and I was asked once again, since I was so successful before, to give the altar call by our director Dr. Calvin White.

We sang our regular set of tunes and I excitedly took the microphone at the end and shared the plan of salvation with the audience, waiting once again for the altars to be filled with crying, passionate people seeking the Lord as their Savior. I just knew it was going to happen again. I expected it and waited for God to move. *Why wouldn't He?* I'm the same guy who gave the altar call a week ago and hundreds came up; why would that change now?

I proceeded to give the altar call, asking people to come forward to accept Christ as their Lord and Savior. I asked once, no one came up. So I reworded the call and asked again. No response. I reworded it yet a third and a fourth time and not one soul came forward to the altar! I was shocked, hurt and quite frankly, my pride was shattered.

What happened?

That evening I roomed with the director in the local hotel. Cal was a mentor and inspiration to me during that time of my life, and I am grateful to this day for his influence on me.

As we prepared to go to sleep, I was still in shock and dismay, that no one responded to the altar call, and Cal knew it. He could tell I was deep in thought over the whole experience. He asked me how I thought it went that night. I responded with a heart filled with amazement as to why no one came forward. He was at the college the weekend before when the altars were full and he had seen the passion of the night. He knew it was a genuine move of God. He saw firsthand the work God did that evening and saw the jubilation of my heart when the people responded. And now he was watching and listening firsthand to the questions I was dealing with because no one had responded. I was the same person that night that I was last week, wasn't I? I thought I was. What happened in that short period of time? What happened to my anointing? Was I really *"called"* by God to do this ministry thing? The questions began rolling out of my heart.

Cal listened and then began to encourage me.

He told me something that night I've never forgotten and remember to this day every time I give an altar call. Cal said, "Your job is not to bring them to the altar. That's the Holy Spirit's job. Your job is to just simply share the message of Truth with them and invite them to come to Jesus. You do your part and if no one responds, that's okay; you did your job. Remember, if no one comes or if thousands come, it's all for the Glory of Jesus Christ, not you."

My entire ministry would never to be the same from that day on. My way of thinking was changed immediately. It was then I realized my attempts to manipulate people into coming down to the altar to give their lives to God that night was nothing but just that, manipulation. I gave four good attempts to manipulate them with the best of my words. After all, I wanted to look good and I wanted to feel successful like I did the weekend before. It was all about my feelings, my reputation and my glory; a trap set by the enemy.

I've now come to the place in my life where I want God to look good when I give an altar call. If no one responds, so be it; I did my part. My heart now is to please God, not man.

Church, instead of putting all the pressure on your pastor or spiritual leaders to do all the work in getting people to come to Christ, how about you begin to do the work of the Church everywhere you go and provide souls with the opportunity to come to Christ? It's not just the job of the so-called clergy; it's your job too! But do it to glorify God, not to glorify you. You do your part and let God do His. And He will. You just obey.

That was a long one, so here's a short one. . .

Let's look at the eleventh contrast between a Kingdom mindset and Church mindset.

11. COMMUNICATION WITH GOD

A Kingdom mindset talks with God and hears from God. A Church mindset just talks to God.

Here's the deal; every devout believer, in fact, any person of faith from any religious persuasion, whether Christian, Muslim, Buddhist, Hindu, or whatever – believes in prayer. However that prayer usually consists of us doing all of the talking. We get a little nervous when someone starts *hearing* from God.

Yes, Kingdom people talk to God, but they are willing to take the time to hear from God as well. Talking is one thing; listening is another. It's time we start listening more to what the Spirit of God is telling us instead of us telling Him what we think. May we all listen more and talk less.

Spiritual manipulators love to pray, especially when others are around to hear them pray. They are good at forming their words, not for the sake of the Father hearing them, but for the sake of the listening ears around them. If we sound good talking to God, then we must be doing well; thus we manipulate our prayers for the sake of acceptance and control.

Can I be honest?

Years ago I can remember getting ready to attend a prayer meeting where there would be a multitude in attendance. It was an all-Church, citywide prayer gathering where a number of us pastors in the city were asked to pray in front of thousands of people represented in the Body of Christ of Cincinnati, the Church that I co-pastored. Before this citywide prayer event, I found myself praying to the Lord that when I stood before the people to pray to Him, I would pray the right words. Does that not sound silly or even perhaps familiar? I was praying to God, asking Him to give me the words I should be praying to Him so I wouldn't be embarrassed while I was praying to Him in front of all those people. I was operating in that crazy old-fashioned Church manipulative mindset.

Here's a little experiment I've been doing lately. You will more than likely be able to recall sitting in a restaurant time and time again with a group of people and someone is expected to pray and bless the meal. Well, when I'm sitting at the table, the person everyone is expecting to pray over the food is usually me. Everyone expects me to pray; after all, I'm a preacher right? I get paid to pray, so why wouldn't I pray over the meal?

It's inevitable. The server brings the food; everyone glances my way, holds hands, closes their eyes, and waits for me to pray. It's then that I'm silent. I don't pray. I keep my eyes open and wait as one at a time people begin opening their eyes to see what's wrong with me and why I'm not praying. I'll wait all night if I have to while the food gets cold until someone steps up to pray. (And the person everyone usually defaults to is Butch!)

As a reminder, don't manipulate when you pray. Just talk to God. Don't put on your "prayer voice" when you're praying in front of others, just use your normal voice. Don't try and come up with these great spiritual words that make you look holy. Who are you trying to impress anyway? In reality, people really don't care about how you sound when you pray. They know that if you're truly a Kingdom minded person, you're praying to God. So just be yourself, with your own voice, using your words and talk to God. And yes, don't forget to listen.

The following movie quote reminds me how we just need to be ourselves and not try to be someone we are not.

Famous Movie Quote:

2010 Movie THE KING'S SPEECH [4]
Lionel Logue: *"You still stammered on the 'W'."*
King George VI: *"Well I had to throw in a few so they knew it was me."*

Stop Your Dependence Upon the Pastor

12. PASTORAL DEPENDENCE

A Kingdom mindset believes the body of Christ is equal and able to minister to one another without cumbersome equations. The Church mindset believes that the pastor must be the one to minister to the body of Christ.

It drives me crazy when the attitude of the body is that the pastor is the one who must do the teaching, the leading, the vision casting, the deliverance maker, the money maker, the all-in-all to all people. We are not! Dependency on the pastor from the Church Body leads to people no longer depending upon God as their source. Instead the pastor becomes the source. Church, we need each other. We are equal. I am no more anointed than you. I have no more authority than you. We are the Body of Christ, *the Church.*

Yes, I have a responsibility as the shepherd to lead, comfort, feed, and equip the sheep; which I take seriously now and forever. But if you are waiting on me or some other clergy member to take care of all of your needs, you are barking up the wrong tree. We

116

can't do it; nor are we supposed to. We, as the body, need to be here for each other through thick and thin, helping, guiding, leading, teaching, and admonishing each other daily! That's a Kingdom mindset.

The problem with many spiritual leaders is the opinion that they have to be the ones to minister to others and no one else is qualified or can. They manipulate others into thinking only they have all the answers and truths, and only they are the ones people must come to for help. When we so-called spiritual leaders begin to manipulate people into thinking that we are the answer to all their problems, we are in a heap of trouble. And when you as the Church begin to depend upon us for all of your answers, you are in a heap of trouble.

Who is the sovereign authority in our lives? The government? No. Man? No. The pastor? No. Our spiritual leaders? No. The sovereign authority in our lives is GOD and GOD alone. He uses His Bride to minister life to one another!

Just how many more of these contrasts are there, Campfield? No worries, just 4 more.

13. LANGUAGE

A Kingdom mindset nurtures leaders who are world changers and "cultural initiators" who articulate truth to society. A Church

117

mindset nurtures leaders who speak religious language relevant only to Church people.

Have you ever noticed our "Christian-eese" language, the way we talk? We have our own language that most unchurched people have no idea what we are saying!

You may or may not recall these lyrics to an old chorus written years ago, Revelation 19:12-16 *"He has fire in His eyes and a sword in His hand. And He's riding a White Horse across this land."* That's an old song that I truly love to sing and I believe in those lyrics. But there's a problem with it when we sing it during a Sunday morning Celebration – the unchurched people will think we're crazy! Now don't get me wrong, I believe the Holy Spirit can and will win over their hearts and give them an understanding and desire for truth that will outweigh our lyrics – but for Pete's sake – let's not make it too weird and difficult for them to understand what we are celebrating!

Have you ever noticed how some people are so full of religious culture they feel like they have to have their eyes closed at all times when they pray? They have to have their eyes closed and hold hands in order to pray (like the restaurant experience I wrote about in contrast number eleven of this chapter). And, you'd better not be wearing a hat! How disrespectful! And preaching in blue jeans – you're not getting anywhere with God in that way. How foolish we have become when we think thoughts like these.

Kingdom mindsets are not full of religious rules that we have to follow – but we are FREE to be who God has called us to be, walking out that freedom in how we pray, what we look like, what we wear, how we share the gospel, how we raise our children, how we respond to our bosses at work, and a multitude of responses in our everyday lives.

Kingdom people have a desire to articulate truth in such a way that it is understandable to the world around them. It is those who desire to manipulate their position that use the holier-than-thou type of language in hopes to impress people with their closeness to God. Yes, they may sound holy and very institutional, but no one can understand what they're really saying! When this happens, **your impact is worthless**!

14. ENEMY LINES

A Kingdom mindset isn't afraid to go behind enemy lines. A Church mindset prays for those who are going behind enemy lines.

Yes, prayer is important for those who are going behind the lines of the enemy's forces, and they need our prayers. But too often we're praying for everyone else and not going ourselves! We've got to have the mindset that we pray - and then we go. We go forth into the ranks of the enemy and do warfare. Jesus came to ignite a fire within you that would consume you. Jesus, the Kingdom Fighter, came to fight for your heart. If He has won your heart, then following your heart will always lead you to follow the heart of God. He will always lead you to advance forward behind enemy lines to win the hearts of those who do not yet know Him or love Him.

It's time to fight; knowing we only have one enemy, and it's not man. It's the devil. We can't be afraid to go to war and fight. Yes pray, and then go! Daily. Go! People are dying and going to hell. It's time to fight. It's time to contend against the enemy with no fear.

A Kingdom mindset will risk it all for the Kingdom of God to come forth. They just don't sit back and pray for those who are risking it all; they risk it all themselves. I have seen numerous Church leaders who stand behind their prayers and talk, but have no action. They will manipulate you into thinking they are on the front lines of the enemy and doing warfare; but behind the scenes, they are pretty comfortable to just sit back and let the so called, *less important* soldiers do the fighting. It's wrong. It's manipulation and must stop. It's time for these spiritual leaders to either put up, or shut up. (Ouch, that sounds pretty harsh doesn't it? We're not allowed to say, "shut up" in our home, but I hope you hear the context of why I write it.) It's one of those Arrrggghhhhh things for me.

Have the cows come home yet?

15. A BUILDING

A Kingdom mindset could care less about the location in which they come together for corporate worship. A Church mindset strives towards owning a building they can call "their own" and making it visible for everyone in the community to see. I pretty much covered this in contrast number two of this chapter, so let's let this be a bit of a refresher. (I could actually preach this till the cows come home; to which some of those cows have come home.)

Church; again, it's not about the building. We *are* the Church. The Church is *not* the building. When we get so caught up about *where* we worship as opposed to *whom* we worship, we will have become a very traditional, Church-minded body of believers and our impact will once again be worth nothing!

I love this quote by JG Davies, "The social location of the church meeting expresses and influences the character of the Church." [5]

If you assume that where the Church gathers is simply a matter of convenience, you are tragically mistaken. You are overlooking a basic reality of humanity. Every building we encounter elicits a response from us. Within its interior and exterior, it explicitly shows us what the church is and how it functions.

You'll notice how churches in the past, (buildings) are built with steeples, high on a hill, with pulpits and pews. A high place (pride). Pulpits and pews (separation of pastor and parishioners). There's no equality and makes the Church look prideful.

In the United States alone, real estate owned by institutional Churches today is worth over $230 billion. Churches have such debt in paying off their buildings that they are unable to truly make the investments for the Kingdom of God in reaching the lost, providing for the needy, feeding the poor, clothing the naked, and doing all those things Jesus requires of us.

Enough said. Cows, come on home.

Last contrast in this chapter. . . finally

The last contrast between a Kingdom mindset and Church mindset. . .

16. SENSITIVITY

A Kingdom mindset is non-compromising and Holy Spirit sensitive. A Church mindset isn't afraid to compromise and nothing but seeker sensitive (or so traditional it is seeker unfriendly).

What does it mean to be totally "seeker sensitive"? That's when we do everything we can to not confront, confuse or offend, etc. those who are seeking after Christ. We don't want to embarrass anyone, thus we go to great extremes to make them feel as comfortable as we possibly can when they're in our midst. It's not just being seeker sensitive in our church buildings, but we're seeker sensitive as *The Church*, the Body of Christ. We have one foot in the world and one in the Kingdom, trying to be "relevant" in every sphere of our lives. That's when we go out of our way to make them "feel comfortable" with us, but we end up compromising our values. Yes, many churches and individuals do that, and that's okay for them, if that's what they choose. I, for one have this heart for my personal family as well as for our Eastgate Community Church family that my bride and I serve. . ..

"That we will be a non-compromising, Holy Spirit driven Church and family, knowing that the Holy Spirit Himself is sensitive to those who are seeking." I don't need to be seeker sensitive; I need to be Holy Spirit sensitive. The Holy Spirit will be sensitive to those who are seeking. So, if I'm being led by the Holy Spirit, then He'll give me the words to say, actions to have, etc. knowing that He cares about those who need Christ even more than I do! **If I'm sensitive to the Holy Spirit, then I'll be sensitive to those who are seeking, because He is even more sensitive to them than I am.**

In my opinion, the Body of Christ has for too long compromised our standards on morality and the Truths of God's Word. We have watered down the gospel, attempting to show ourselves so relevant to society in our services and individual lives, that we have placed ourselves in the realm of having one foot in the world and one in the Lord – which we cannot do! Nor will God allow us to do so. The Father expects us to live a life that is Worthy of who He is! – Not of who we are!

Sadly, I've encountered some spiritual leaders who have manipulated the Holy Spirit right out of who they are and what they do. They are so busy trying not to offend others that they end up offending the Holy Spirit. They'll do everything they can to manipulate "their people" into being so sensitive to the world they end up manipulating them to ignore the presence of the Holy Spirit in their lives.

Arrrggghhhhh!

Are you done with this yet? Yes, almost.

Let me wrap up this chapter. Wow. I've given you lot to chew on. I understand as well that some of this may be controversial to your mindset and your upbringing, which is okay. It's taken me years to get out of the old traditional Church mindset I've grown up in all my life. Being raised in a strong Christian home, I understand the values of that upbringing and thank the Lord for it. But through the course of time, I have found that some of the things I do in my relationship with God as it relates to the Church, I've been doing simply out of tradition and comfort. I've been doing it for so long, speaking it for so long, living it for so long, that I just keep doing it over and over, thus it has become an old Church mindset.

It's time to change our mindsets. It's time to realize that some of the things we've been doing are not Biblical and that God is moving in fresh and new ways. It's time to move forward, investing in the Kingdom of God with Kingdom mindsets, eliminating the manipulative influence over people to do anything other than living the Kingdom way of life.

It's time we started living our lives with a Kingdom mindset – not a traditional Church mindset as is the typical mindset of many Christians today. If we truly want to invest for eternity, having this Kingdom mindset is of the utmost importance!

Time to Get Real. . .

1. Identify the differences between a Kingdom mindset and the traditional Church mindset.
2. Jesus asked the question, "Why do you yourselves transgress the commandment of God for the sake of your _____?
3. Do you think it's easy for people to break out of the old traditional Church mindset of life? Why or why not?
4. What are some personal tips you could share from your experience in how you have broken out of the old Church mindset?
5. What's the harm of staying in that traditional mindset? Which do you feel is the easier mindset to have, the old Church one or a Kingdom one?

6. What do you do when everyone around you has the traditional Church mindset and you're trying to live your life under a Kingdom mindset?

7. Share some examples of traditional habits that you want to or need to change.

8. What does it mean to "test and approve" God's will?

Chapter 6

"Characteristics of a Religious Spirit"

"Characteristics of a Religious Spirit"

*I*n my experience in dealing with people who are spiritual manipulators and abusers, they seem to have a lot of things in common, one of which is having a religious spirit. A religious spirit or attitude almost always accompanies someone who is a manipulative and controlling individual. If we, as the Body of Christ, are taught what to look for and if we can identify certain characteristics found in the lives of those who are attempting to manipulate us, we'll be one step ahead of the game. We will be able to fly higher and quicker, making an even greater impact for the Kingdom of God. The Church must have a knowledge of what God's Word teaches us so that we are not caught unaware of the schemes of the devil, our great adversary, the author of a religious spirit.

WARNING!

Before I go any further, I feel compelled to warn you to watch out that you are not found guilty of entertaining a religious, manipulative spirit yourself by trying to identify those you think are entertaining one. The enemy could use this as a vicious trap to keep you from walking in your own freedom from these spirits.

In this chapter, we are going to look at the characteristics of a religious spirit and how to identify whether or not you are possibly entertaining this spirit yourself. It is a religious spirit that helps to keep one in the old traditional Church mindset. It is the ugly religious spirit that works side by side with a spirit of manipulation found within the ranks of the Body of Christ. These spirits must be dealt with if we're going to soar. And soar we will!

Throughout this chapter I will be sharing a portion of the teachings from Os Hillman in his book, *"The Religious Spirit and Spiritual Strongholds in the Workplace"* [1], C. Peter Wagner's book, *"Freedom from the Religious Spirit"* [2], as well as teachings of my own. It is my heart's desire to provide insight into this demonic spirit. This demonic spirit can destroy from the inside out as its forms of manipulation tear at the very fabric of the modern day Kingdom Minded Church, thus leaving a path of death and destruction in its wake, making the Body of Christ weak and powerless. This is not the way God intended for the Church to be. He intended for us to walk with great anointing, clarity, strength, purity, and fresh revelation of who *He* is and who He has called *us* to be – *The Church*.

Let's dive into this, shall we?

Let me ask you this question: Do you have an Authentic Kingdom Mindset or Imitation Kingdom Mindset? There will be those who will attempt to convince you into believing that they have a Kingdom mindset, but through the smoke and mirrors of the devil, you will find a religious spirit that is manipulating, harassing, intimidating, leading, and directing this person's life for the sake of control, deceit, and the breeding of the old traditional Church mindset.

You don't have to be "demon possessed" to be influenced by a religious spirit. Though there are those in the world today who are possessed by demons; those co-operating with a religious spirit are more plentiful. You don't have to be possessed, but you may be influenced by these spirits in your decision making process. It's like the old cartoon of the devil sitting on the shoulder of a person speaking things into their ear to get them to make certain decisions.

The Definition of a Religious Spirit

Dr. Peter Wagner defines the religious spirit as. . . "An agent of Satan assigned to prevent change and maintain the status quo by using religious devices." [3]

The religious spirit seeks to distort a genuine move of God through deception, control, and manipulation. This spirit operates out of old religious structures and attempts to maintain the status quo, favoring tradition over a genuinely intimate relationship with God. It influences believers to live the Christian life based on works instead of grace. Similar to the Greek way of thinking, the religious spirit depends on human effort to acquire spiritual knowledge and favor from God.

Keep This In Mind

In the years before the Protestant Reformation, Martin Luther's greatest challenge was to root out the religious spirit. He was told by his religious teachers there were stringent requirements for receiving the favor of God. We see this as they write to him the following. . .

"Remember Martin, just to pray by yourself is not enough. The church has to pray for you too. Even when the priest has asked that you be forgiven, God will not listen unless you do good works. The more gifts you give to the church and to the poor, the more trips you make to Rome and Jerusalem, the more pleasures you give up, the better will be your chances for heaven. The best and safest way to do all this, and the one that is most God pleasing, is to give up everything and become a monk."[4]

The essence of Martin Luther's struggle to win God's favor still resides in many Christians today.

Take note: The voice of the religious spirit is found in dead and spiritually lifeless Churches all over the world. But do not be deceived; religious spirits are not limited to any particular denomination. The religious spirit can be heard loud and clear, even in the most prolific Church.

I have been in many Church services that seemed to have their act together. In one particular Church where I knew the pastor personally, the congregation was large, the music was rockin' and the staff seemed to have everything going for them. The preacher spoke with the articulation of a master orator full of truth and wisdom, while the listeners listened intently with the desire to learn. The musicians were the best in the business. They didn't miss a beat and the praise team could sing the lights out! The Church seemed like the answer for the community - and they were in a lot of ways. However, the leaders were skilful in their manipulations through the mask and mirrors of deception. Even though the intent of the staff and congregation was filled with purity, the core of the Church was filled with abusive manipulation.

Keep in mind the battle we are in as stated in 2 Corinthians 10:4-5 *"The weapons we fight with are not the weapons of the world. On the contrary, they have divine power to demolish strongholds. We demolish arguments and every pretension that sets itself up against the knowledge of God, and we take captive every thought to make it obedient to Christ."*

For our struggle is not against flesh and blood, but against the rulers, against the authorities, against the powers of this dark world and against the spiritual forces of evil in the heavenly realms. Ephesians 6:12

We must realize we are not dealing with flesh and blood when we deal with a religious spirit. The religious spirit deceives believers into thinking that the only way to get God's approval is through works. It nullifies the importance of faith and grace that has been given to them through the work of the Cross.

In a letter to Timothy, the Apostle Paul warns his spiritual son about religious spirits and gives him implicit instructions about how to interact with them. Scripture says in 2 Timothy 3:5, *"Having a form of godliness, but denying the power thereof: from such turn away."* As Paul so matter-of-factly points out, religious spirits have a "form of godliness" – they appear religious but lack the spiritual substance of an intimate believer.

Rick Joyner, of Morning Star Ministries says this about a religious spirit, *"This spirit is the counterfeit to the true love of God, and true worship. This evil spirit has probably done far more damage to the church than the New Age movement and all other cults combined."* [5]

I truly believe that the degree to which we have been delivered from this powerful deception will directly affect the degree to which we will be able to preach the True gospel in True power making a Kingdom Impact in our culture and removing the obstacle of manipulation in carrying this out. If this spirit is not confronted quickly, it will do more damage to the Church, our ministries, our families, and our lives, than possibly any other assault we might suffer.

Here's Another Question. . .

QUESTION: How do you know the difference between the authentic and imitation Kingdom mindsets? How do you know if it's the real deal or a fake?

In order to answer this question, we have to look at the characteristics of a religious spirit, that I've collected from numerous sources [6] as well as my own of which I now present ten of them in no particular order. Once we understand these characteristics, then we are better able to distinguish the difference between real or fake, which will give us an advantage in not only dealing with a spirit of religion but also those manipulative spirits that work hand in hand with it.

10 Characteristics of a Religious Spirit

1. POWERLESSNESS

Having a form of godliness, but denying the power thereof: from such turn away. 2 Timothy 3:5 (KJV)

The Bible is clear that we will be known by our fruit. If a person's life is not bearing fruit for the Kingdom of God, then more than likely they are not a Kingdom-minded person and walking with a worldly mindset. People with a religious spirit will talk the talk like crazy, but when it comes down to actually having any power in their lives, it is non-existent. They can manipulate with great strength and power, but have no power to speak of for the Kingdom of God.

They can talk all day about laying hands on the sick, but they don't do it. They can talk all day about how to change a culture, but they don't do it. They are all talk and no action. The reason they don't do it, is because they've tried in the past and no results occurred, so they quit trying; but they keep talking! A person with no power in their life is more than likely walking with a religious spirit; especially if they are talking the power game but not living the power game.

Super Duper

This kind of person kind of reminds me of our dog Duper who lived with us for her entire 16 years. She was the cutest little dog on the planet, especially if she knew you. If she knew you when you came to the door, she would look at you with sweet little eyes and walk away with her informal gesture of acceptance and leave you alone. However, if she didn't know you when you came to the door, she would give you a "bark" lashing. Her little bark was harsh and sounded like she could tear into you at any moment. But she never did. For 16 years, she would bark with the crisp and clear intent as if she was going to bite into a stranger. But it never happened. She was all bark and no bite. That's the way a person walking with a religious spirit is - all bark and no bite. They'll talk it, but they have nothing to back it up.

2. NEGATIVE, CYNICAL, AND HYPERCRITICAL

A person with a religious spirit seems to always focus on the negative things that are happening around them. It's their tendency to see as their primary mission the tearing down that which others believe. The religious spirit has an inclination to see more of what is wrong with other people or other Churches than what is right with them.

This type of person reminds me of a character that one of my pastors and mentors used to refer to when he was preaching;

"Sister Sand Paper." Sister Sand Paper was the lady in the Church that would rub everyone raw. She was itchy, scratchy, abrasive, and negative with every lash of her tongue. Religious people are like Sister Sand Paper. Whenever you get around them, you can count on them to open up a wound or hurt through their negative, cynical, abrasive, manipulative attitudes with every word that comes out of their mouths.

A religious spirit is joyless, cynical, and hypercritical. This can turn a home, a Church, Christian organization, or company completely sour. Then, whenever genuine joy and love are expressed, this becomes a threat to those who have lost the simplicity of true faith in what they believe.

Religious spirits are critical. No one can do anything for God better than they. Their ideas and ways of doing God's work is the "right way" because God has spoken to them directly. Religious spirits constantly play "The God Card" acknowledging that if God were to talk to anyone, it would be them, and certainly not you! No matter what you do or how you do God's work, remember, according to religious spirits, it could have been done better! **Wow, talk about manipulative!**

Religious spirits rarely start or carry through on anything of their own accord. They will, however, talk about how poorly you do it. A great deal of time is spent talking about what great and magnificent things they are going to do for God, while simultaneously criticizing what you are actively doing for Him. In reality, they often do little outside of their own imaginations. Watch out for the "but" statements from a religious person because it's the springboard to criticism. Beware of the critical religious spirit with an imagined ministry that has not yet materialized. Avoid the critics; work with the workers and not with the talkers.

3. HOLY CORRECTION AND PERFECTIONISM

This is someone who is always trying to fix what's wrong with other people, as if God Himself appointed them with this mission. As we've stated, these spirits of religion and manipulation work hand in hand. What's interesting about a religious spirit is that, even though they know it all, they are often unwilling to jump in and help unless the task brings them some recognition. Religious people often tell you how to do what they are unwilling to do themselves, and manipulate you into doing it for them.

Oftentimes a spirit of perfectionism accompanies a religious spirit. Perfectionism is an extreme behaviour or expectation beyond the balance of being excellent. It is often impracticable, extremely time consuming, and because performance standards are raised so high, the work never gets started, finished, or measures up to the perfectionist's standards. That is why the religious perfectionists seldom accomplish much beyond frustrating themselves or criticism of others.

One thing I've learned through the years of ministry is that if we had to do everything just perfect, then nothing would ever get done. I am not saying we should not maintain a standard of excellence in ministry. We just need to guard ourselves from the polarization of religious perfectionism.

I knew a lady on a Church staff who was a perfectionist. Everything she did had to be just right. Everything had to be perfect in every way and until it was perfect, she would not present it to her team. Her team eventually became despondent. Having to wait for her to give them what they needed to do their jobs created great frustration. The team members eventually quit, one by one. The frustration of waiting for perfection was a recipe for disaster. Still, the Church staff member did not change her ways. Her philosophy was that if it was going to be done, then it had to be done right; and if it couldn't be done right, then it wouldn't be done at all.

Sadly, there are many of us who have that same attitude. Church, yes, do your job with excellence. Serve with the heart of excellence for the King of kings, Jesus Christ. But don't do it with an attitude that spoils things for everyone around you. If it's not perfect, that's okay; just give it your best. After all, none of us are perfect, but God still chooses to use us.

The fourth characteristic of a Religious Spirit is. . .

4. DECREE AND FLEE

Religious spirits don't take hints and cannot handle Spirit-led confrontations. Their motto is "decree and flee." They flee when exposed, and decree how unloving and unconcerned you are as they go to the next unsuspecting Church or organization. They decree how you should be living your life, your ministry, and family. Then flee the scene with no accountability involved.

I have watched ministry leaders try to deal with, and correct ever so gently, these religious spirits - to no avail. They try to make you afraid to say anything to them at all because you never know how they may react. You feel like you're walking on eggshells around them. Just go ahead and break the shells because religious spirits usually can't take subtle hints; they must be confronted head on. Be humble of heart, without malice, innocent as a dove, gentle in your heart, but bold as a lion. **Breaking that attitude of religion and manipulation may be tough, but with God, it can be done!**

Speaking of those who decree and flee, I've met some of those old time evangelists who say things like, "I don't have to live here, so I'm just going to tell you how it is and let the pastor clean it up later." They manipulate, decree, and flee. No heart for the sheep, just an expression of their religious attitude should be enough, with no questions asked. I can't stand it.

Arrrggghhhhh!

5. SPIRITUAL COMPARING

This is when we have the tendency to compare ourselves to others we think are less spiritual, thus building up ourselves while tearing others down. A religious spirit becomes prideful and isolated, thinking that his or her righteousness is special and that he or she cannot associate with other believers who have different or lesser standards. Churches that allow these attitudes become elitist—and dangerously vulnerable to deception or cult-like practices.

A Religious Know-It-All Attitude

Religious and manipulative spirits are seldom teachable because they think they already know it all. Whether or not the person has ever had any actual first-hand experience with the business at hand is of no matter. They may not have the first clue how to organize a banquet, for example, but they are quite sure you are not doing it right, and are even more certain they could do a better job if they were only given the opportunity. It doesn't matter what the activity is, the person with a religious spirit always thinks he/she knows more than you do.

This "know-it-all" attitude results in religious spirits becoming offended by anyone who they perceive may know more than they do. I speak from experience. I tried to become friends with a pastor in our city after a series of meetings together. With each encounter, I began to realize this guy had one of those know-it-all attitudes. He wanted to give everyone the impression in the room he had the answers. He was young and raw to the ministry, and it was quite evident. The more time I spent in his presence, the more I wanted

141

to get out of his presence. His attitude of knowing everything was repulsive to my spirit, and more than likely, everyone else in the room as well.

If someone tried to confront him regarding his attitude, he would walk away from that relationship and find someone who would agree with him. He didn't take confrontation well at all. He ended up walking out of my life too. Apparently, his friendship with me wasn't worth the grief it caused him. Eventually, he found a group of people just like him, and thus he's happy. Or is he? Who really knows?

Hopefully we are always open to be taught, explore better strategies, and ways of doing things. Unfortunately, most of the time a person with a religious spirit's advice is only a facade for self-righteousness, legalism, criticism, and manipulation.

Godly Elitism falls into this category as well. Having a sense that we are closer to God than other people or that our lives and ministries are more pleasing to God, is an attitude of Godly Elitism. A religious spirit develops a harsh, judgmental attitude toward sinners, yet those who ingest this poison typically struggle with sinful habits they cannot admit to anyone else.

The Fancy Side of Life

I am reminded of a time in our lives we were between homes. The home we were living in had a toxic mold growing in the crawl space under the house, causing us to have to move out and destroy our possessions. Until we found a more permanent place to live, we moved into a vacant friend's home in a neighborhood that was much different from what we were used to. The previous neighborhood was friendly, kind, and sweet. The neighbors would all talk to each other while our dogs would affectionately lick each other with joy. Everyone would wave as they passed one another in their cars along the roadside. The kids could play outside with no fear of harm and everyone looked out for each other. Our neighbors would watch our home when we were gone and we would keep an eye on theirs when they were gone. It was like living in Mayberry with Andy and Barnie.

Then suddenly, as we moved into this new home, into this new neighborhood, we had a reality check! Though not true in reality, but true in my perspective, the neighborhood seemed like it was quite wealthy, with everyone driving fancy, expensive cars and living in multi-million dollar homes. No one seemed to care you were there. If you passed a neighbor while going for a walk, there would never be an exchange of pleasantries. Not even a "How ya doing?" It seemed as if people would rarely talk to each other, let alone allow our dogs to exchange licks with each other. It was as if everyone was too good for everyone else, so everyone just stuck to him or herself and stayed in their own little circles of high-class living.

The people in that new neighborhood seemed to rarely interact with anyone that didn't live their lifestyle. It was as if they didn't want to be tainted by outsiders. This parallels with the reality that religious people rarely interact with nonbelievers because they don't want their own superior morals to be tainted by them.

Now, before I move on, please forgive my seemingly judgmental attitude toward the people in that neighborhood. In reality to what I now know, for the most part, they are wonderful loving people who love their families and are making a great impact in our city in many positive ways. In fact, a large majority of them are believers in Christ and a part of the overall Church in Cincinnati in which I co-pastor. My initial impression of them was wrong and judgmental, not unlike a person who entertains a religious spirit: tending to be judgmental and not wanting anything to do with someone who is beneath their class or way of spiritual life. I actually came to love and appreciate some of the people in the neighborhood; they befriended us in our time of need. I have found them to be some of the sweetest people I have had the privilege of knowing.

Polished People

Religious spirits are polished. They can be the most polite people (at least in public) you could ever meet. But remember this; words of deception, spoken with flattering lips, are still words of deception. For example, I remember this one sharp pastor friend of mine. He wore the best suits and fancy shoes one could buy. GQ would have welcomed him! He could speak like the President giving the State of the Union Address and had everyone following him. He was polished. However, knowing him personally, I witnessed his methods of manipulation and deceit.

People with religious spirits will continue to display their suave facade until they find out their smooth words are not effective in controlling or manipulating you. Then their tune will change. If gentility doesn't work, then the "God told me to tell you" card will often manifest. The problem is that God is always telling them you should stick with their traditions and, of course, you had better listen! It is interesting to note that they always hear God speaking about your faults, but never hear the disclosure of their own faults. Right!

Here's an ugly characteristic – as if they're not all ugly

6. JEALOUS, GOSSIPY, SNOOPS

This is the tendency to be suspicious of or to oppose new movements, Churches, or ministries. A religious spirit persecutes those who disagree with their self-righteous views and becomes angry whenever the message of grace threatens to undermine their religiosity. An angry religious person, full of jealousy, will use gossip and slander to assassinate other peoples' characters and may even use violence to prove his or her point as they manipulate their way through the destruction of lives.

Religious Gossips

Webster defines a gossip as *"a person who chatters or repeats idle talk and rumors, especially about the private affairs of others."* [7] With such a critical nature, religious spirits find plenty about which to gossip. These gossipy spirits are always looking for and talking about the faults of others. They are the ones with the beams in their eyes, but all they can see is the speck in yours (Matthew 7:3). People with religious, manipulative spirits tend to look at themselves through rose-coloured glasses, while looking at everyone else under a microscope. Gossip is the destructive weapon of these spirits.

Gossip is a marked characteristic of these spirits. They are critical talebearers and evil tattletales. You can spot gossipy religious spirits in the back of the church, hallways, bathrooms, parking lots, or in the side rooms of your meeting place. They'll find their way to the water cooler quicker than anyone. Like birds of a feather they flock together. Religious spirits hang out with and are drawn to, one another to assassinate others with their tongues. After Church services and meetings with other Christians, they can't wait to reach for their cell phones, online chat rooms, and e-mails. They will fill their Facebook [8] page with all kinds of gossip, but do it in a way that makes them look good, all the while on the attack. They will often do it by quoting particular scriptures in the Bible that will fill their gossip gun with the ammunition they need to appear holy and above the fray.

Religious Snoops

Religious snoops will go out of their way to chase down rumors and pry into things that are surely none of their business. They hope to uncover juicy morsels of information that can be used as a slanderous weapon.

7. THE HUNT FOR POSITION

Position seeking is one of the most obvious characteristics of the religious spirit. The religious spirit is always looking to advance into positions of influence and visibility in the church through their manipulative ways so they can fulfil their purpose: to be admired by others.

Since religious spirits are interested in status, titles and positions; they often select Churches whose pastors appear to have great potential and will allow them to advance their own ministry.

Within our Cincinnati area, I have observed a particular group of people move from Church to Church over the years. These people try to worm their way into the hearts of the leadership, hoping to be accepted into the ranks. When it does not happen, they bolt and try the next Church. If it wasn't so sad, it might be comical. They are never satisfied and are always looking for something they will never attain until they repent of their ways and approach Church life with a spirit of humility, love, and purity.

People with religious spirits want to know what is in it for them? How can they achieve recognition, visibility, position, and honor within the local Church? Then they will commit themselves to the vision of the house. But these motives are contrary to the Word of God. Job 32:21-22 says, *"Let me not, I pray you, accept any man's person, neither let me give flattering titles unto man. For I know not to give flattering titles; in so doing my maker would soon take me away."*

Titles, of course, are necessary because they help us define job descriptions and areas of responsibility in our society. To seek titles, however, with the intent of exercising religious control, or to seek a leadership position to gain man's admiration, is truly unrighteousness and is the activity of a religious spirit. Titles given only to flatter, manipulate, or control someone are not biblical and ultimately lead to confusion and trouble.

Sometimes titles are offered as a form of religious control as well. Sometimes a disgruntled Church member is offered the title and position of a leader by the pastor just to keep him from leaving the Church. The evangelist who greets a pastor by preceding his name with a flattering and fashionable title in hopes of booking a meeting is also in the hunt for position. The dissatisfied choir member who is ready to leave is given a solo in the next Christmas Experience with a desire they'll stay and continue to sing on Sundays. These manipulative tactics simply feed the prideful nature of the religious.

8. A "LOOK AT ME NOW" DESIRE

Doing things in order to be noticed and accepted by men fulfills the "Look at me now" desire. A religious spirit places emphasis on doing *outward* things to show others that God accepts him or her. We deceive and manipulate ourselves into believing we can win God's approval through a religious dress code, certain spiritual disciplines, particular music styles, or even doctrinal positions.

Most of the time the religious spirits try to appear righteous in public. They will say things in front of others that tend to exalt their religious posture or social status, unlike Pastor Moses who I talked about in the introduction of this book. This was a man who was knee deep in religion and manipulation and did everything he could to give the impression he was the man of the hour with the desire to be accepted by not only his own people, but myself, a visiting guest from another country.

9. PAST GLORIFICATION

Past glorification is glorying more in what God has done in the past than what He is doing in the present. The focus is on the past and our future is aborted. A religious spirit rejects progressive revelation and refuses to embrace change. This is why many Churches become irrelevant to society. They become so focused on what God did fifty years ago that they become stuck in a time warp—and cannot move forward when the Holy Spirit begins to speak in new ways. When religious groups refuse to shift with God's new directives, they become "old wineskins"; God must find more flexible vessels that are willing to implement His changes.

Who's keeping score?

10. KEEPING SCORE

This characteristic drives us to keep score of our spiritual lives. Because we go to more meetings, read our Bibles more, or do more things for the Lord than most other Christians, we can feel better about ourselves and have a "higher score."

A religious spirit views God as a cold, harsh, distant taskmaster rather than an approachable, loving Father. When we base our relationship with God on our ability to perform spiritual duties, we deny the power of grace. God does not love us because we pray, read our Bibles, attend church, or witness. Yet millions of Christians think God is mad if they don't perform these and other duties perfectly. As a result they struggle to find true intimacy with Jesus.

I Almost Blew It
Actually, I did blow it!

Butch and I had left our youth pastorate in Montana and had moved back to Washington. We were only a few years into the ministry and I felt like I had to do everything I could to not only make points with the local people in our Church, but also with our denomination. Therefore, I would attempt to get involved in everything I could to prove to the powers that be that I was indeed worthy of promotion in their sight. I was involved with our local church gatherings, city gatherings, and district gatherings within our denomination, as well as national gatherings. I tried to do it all.

I volunteered for everything I could and gave myself whole-heartedly to the ministry at hand. I thought I was *"all that."* I played my saxophone before thousands in large gatherings. I built the local youth ministry into a large group of young people who loved God and was ready to take on the world. Seemingly, I had success, but I almost lost my family in the process. I allowed a reli-gious, manipulative spirit to begin to take over. Thus my priorities became distorted from the way God originally planned for my life. I thought I was scoring points with everyone, but little did I know at the time I was losing points with the ones I loved the most. . . my family and my God.

My priorities were totally out of whack; I made some bad deci-sions. I was deceived into thinking I was untouchable and pride set into my heart. The decisions I made put not only my ministry in jeopardy but my marriage as well. I was succeeding in every area of my life except for my personal home life. Butch and I became more and more distant from each other, and the enemy tried to destroy the covenant we had made with God and each other. If not for the grace of God and a loving and forgiving wife, I would have lost my family. Thankfully they forgave me, loved me, worked with me and together we have become what we are today - a loving couple who love each other passionately and have a passion for God's Presence which infiltrates us daily.

Keeping score to see how many points I could get with others was prideful, abusive, manipulative, and sinful. I was wrong and living in sin. But praise God for His grace and faithfulness.

I stepped out of the vocational full time ministry for a period of time to get help, to learn how to be a proper husband, and man of God. We moved into a small two-roomed apartment in the University of Washington area of Seattle with our two-year-old daughter, Cazi and started life over again. We slept on the floor, ate our meals in the bedroom/kitchen space and used the local bathroom down the hall. I got a job in a door factory sanding and painting doors. At the beginning, I hated every minute of that so-called "secular" job. I thought it was demeaning that I, a man of God, had to lower myself to do such menial labor. Boy did I learn a valuable lesson!

Every day I would wake up and go to the job site to sand and paint those doors. I started each day in prayer and the reading of the Word in my truck. During my breaks I would read the scripture, listen to worship music, and write in my journal. It was in that journal that I penned the words of a young man who was hurting from his very core. The suffering and pain I had inflicted upon my family during my season of manipulation, deceit, and pride was overwhelming. It took me a long time to forgive myself for allowing anything to step between my Butch and I.

I felt my anointing was being wasted and squandered while I sanded and painted doors. Little did I realize, that while I was sanding and painting those doors, God was developing my anointing, fathering, and marriage to be greater than I could have imagined. He knew exactly what He was doing. While I was trying to manipulate others into feeling sorry for me and taking my side, He was busy changing my heart, motives, and desires. He was molding this vessel . . . through the fire . . . into a beautiful and delightful instrument to be used for His Glory.

When I finally got through my pity party, I began to realize the destiny God had in store for Butch and me. The true nature of God's love and mercy was revealed to us. He showed us the reality of His unconditional love and the passion He had for us. It turned out that some of our greatest and fondest memories came as a result of living in that small two-room apartment in the U Dub

District. What the devil meant for bad, God truly turned into good for His Glory!

From that process at the door factory, I learned there are people in life who work hard in their jobs; they love Jesus and have accepted their place of work as their Kingdom Assignment. They understand that their Kingdom Assignment does not have to be decorated in pews and crosses. I learned there are people who sit in the pews on Sunday and look the part, but go to work on Monday and have to face the trials of life that I never experienced before. Working at the door factory gave me a greater love and appreciation for people like I'd never had before. All of my life I've been surrounded with God fearing, loving Christian people who seemed to be blessed. The door factory showed me that there is more to life than what happens within the four walls of the church building. God showed me first hand that the *real* Church is *outside* the walls of the physical church.

It was during that time I truly fell in love with my bride and began to experience what constitutes true sacrifice and dedication. Butch and I became more dependent upon God during that season of our lives than we ever had before. We learned that God was and had to be our only source to which we would turn. I learned as well that she had to be the first priority of my life outside of God. If I didn't honor, cherish, take care of, bless and protect her, then I couldn't expect the blessings of God to be upon our family or me. I learned how to be the covenant spiritual leader in our home.

Now all of that sounds good, doesn't it? But don't let me fool you. **It wasn't an overnight experience that suddenly turned everything around.** We experienced months of long sleepless nights, trying to rest our heads upon tear-stained pillows. We battled each other, and we battled Satan. We battled our flesh and went toe to toe with the darkness of the enemy who attempted to destroy us. It was tough. We give thanks to the Lord for putting people into our lives that walked along side of us. Pastor Bob Smith will forever be our hero for standing with us during our darkest hours. He co-officiated our wedding along with Pastor Bill King in Bend, Oregon in August of 1980. Pastor Bob was my pastor as a young boy; he mentored me and showed me how to be a man of God. He not only stood with me as a boy, but he stood with me as a man. He, along with our families, stood alongside us with encouragement, prayers and unconditional love. These groups of people believed in us and didn't give up on us. They knew the potential we had for the Kingdom of God and did everything in their power to see us succeed.

The Story Gets Even Better

When I got to the point in my life where I accepted the fact that I may never again be in the vocational ministry of a local Church, getting paid to do what I loved; God showed up with His hand of favor and blessings, and changed my course again. I can remember that feeling of knowing God wanted to use me, and I got to the point (though it took a while) that I was content in knowing my ministry was not limited to the stereotypical pastoral role in a "*church*" setting.

God led me to start a Bible study each morning before the workday started by giving me favor with the owners. The owners not only attended the study, but they stressed strongly that all of the employees attend as well. I was in charge of the study and led men to God right there on the work site. My confidence in God grew, as well as my confidence in myself, knowing who God had called me to be. Then as if on cue, God provided a way for us to meet Dr. Mike and Colleen Murray in Cincinnati, Ohio. It was this couple that embraced us, loved us, encouraged us, and believed in us as they invited us to join their Church staff full time.

Through the course of interviews, prayers, and seeking the wisdom of God, we made the decision to leave our home state, friends, and family, to accept their offer to come to Cincinnati to serve alongside them in the local Church as youth, music, and children's pastors. We had come full circle. But this time it was different. I had learned from previous experiences to spot the traps of the enemy and how to stay clear of them. I had learned the pitfalls of abusing, manipulating, and controlling others for my own gain. I had learned that my family was, is, and shall forever be the priority of my life along with God. I wasn't the same person moving to Cincinnati that I was while living in Washington where our marriage was almost destroyed.

Listen Church! Keeping score, comparing ourselves to others, trying to make points in the lives of others by manipulating them and walking with a religious spirit isn't worth it. It never will be! Stop keeping score of what you do; stop thinking God is a task-master expecting you to DO things *for* Him and just fall in love *with* Him. That's what I did and it's working out pretty well for us now. Thank you Lord!

Let's wrap this up shall we? Or shan't we? We shall.

The fact is, there will be those who will make you want to believe they have a Kingdom mindset, but through the smoke and mirrors of the devil, you'll find a religious spirit that is manipulating, harassing, intimidating, leading, and directing this person's life for the sake of control, deceit, and intimidation; thus breeding the old traditional Church mindset. That's what happened to me. Your job is to make sure you are not walking as one who is entertaining the religious spirit, and to make certain that you, as a member of the Body of Christ, do not allow yourself to be manipulated by those who do.

It's not an easy task to always discern this, but you can do it! Be the Church and walk with the confidence given to you by God. And for Pete's sake, do not, I repeat, do not allow yourself to walk in FEAR of those who try to religiously manipulate you. Greater is The God who lives within you than the enemy who lives out there in this world! No Fear!

Even if you don't know exactly what it is you are doing, walk with confidence. Which reminds me of the quote in the SCHOOL OF ROCK movie when Jack Black (playing Dewey Finn) is speaking to the principal. . .

Famous Movie Quote:

2003 Movie SCHOOL OF ROCK [9]
Dewey Finn: *"I'm a teacher. All I need are minds for molding."*

Time to Get Real. . .

The following is a quick self-assessment checklist from Os Hillman and Dr. C. Peter Wagner [10] that you can use to reveal the influence of the Religious Spirit's involvement in your life. They give a list of 25 things to look for; I've narrowed it down to a few less than that. Place a check by any item with which you can identify and see how you line up. When you finish, share your results with someone and tell them how those results make you feel right now.

Religious Spirit Self-Assessment

o You believe your faith life should remain separate from your work life.

o You're motivated to share Christ out of duty.

o You can't relate to non-believers because you're afraid of rejection.

o You display a "better than they are" attitude toward nonbelievers.

o You are viewed by others as dogmatic and rigid (not simply a person of conviction).

o You feel compelled to be involved in religious activity and you can't relax in your faith.

o You often feel guilty (not the same as the conviction of the Holy Spirit) for not sharing Christ with others.

o You often engage in religious debate.

o You need a packaged presentation in order to share the gospel.

o When talking about spiritual matters to strangers, you tend to talk about your church or ask about their church involvement versus talking about Jesus and their personal relationship with God.

o You have a difficult time socializing, loving or accepting those who do not believe the way you do.

o You are motivated by your church leadership out of guilt and Christian duty instead of loving devotion to Christ.

o You discourage change, preferring religious tradition.

o You believe that the ministry gifts listed in 1 Corinthians 12 and 14 and Ephesians 4:11 are no longer applicable today; or, if you believe they are valid, you think that they are for religious professionals, not for you.

o You form relationships for the purpose of achieving a religious activity rather than developing community from which Christ-like ministry flows naturally.

o Your loyalty to denominational structures is greater than your commitment to the kingdom of God and the entire Body of Christ.

o You don't see the need to work with other Christian ministry groups in a common effort; you usually feel that your way is the primary way and everyone should join your endeavor so as not to compromise your belief or doctrine.

So, how did you do? Want to go to the next step?

If you feel you have been affected by a religious spirit, here's a great prayer I would encourage you to say.[11] Please don't just read it in a repetitious way, but say it from your heart.

Prayer of Freedom from a Religious Spirit

Dear Jesus,

I repent and renounce every opening, known and unknown in my personal life that I have given to a religious spirit and every work of darkness connected with it. I repent and renounce every opening, known or unknown of the previous generations in my family that have been given to a religious spirit in my family line. I take authority over those generational spirits, repenting for and renouncing them in Jesus name. I repent for allowing myself to be led by any other spirit than the Holy Spirit.

I repent and renounce placing man's opinion of me above Yours.

I repent and renounce compromises of the truth, of my integrity, and of my purity.

I repent and renounce all compromises in my attitude toward sin.

I repent for my lack of transparency for covering sin, for not confessing sin, for not receiving correction for being defensive and quick to justify and rationalize my sin.

I repent and renounce all deception and hypocrisy.

I repent and renounce all pride, arrogance and self-righteousness.

I repent and renounce all comparison, judgment, criticism, gossip, jealousy, covetousness, and anger.

I repent and renounce all persecution and slander of those moving in the Holy Spirit.

I repent and renounce every act of rebellion that has reinforced the Spirit of Religion in my life.

I choose to have obedience as my heart attitude.

I choose to no longer partner with the same spirit that killed Jesus and that continues to attempt to kill the work of the Holy Spirit today.

I choose to no longer oppose God.

I break every hex, curse or vow, every spell, incantation, or ritual.

I break every covenant and blood covenant, every sacrifice and blood sacrifice.

I break every ungodly soul tie, every ungodly generational tie in my family line.

I break any other legal right, known or unknown, for the Spirit of Religion to stay.

Spirit of religion, as the Body of Christ, I and those with me come against you.

We refuse to allow you to steal our intimate relationship with our Lord.

We refuse to allow you to kill the flow of the Holy Spirit in us.

We refuse to allow you to destroy the anointing of others through us.

We choose to receive the anointing to break the power of the spirit of religion in the Church of Jesus Christ in the name of the Lord Jesus Christ of Nazareth.

Father God, I invite You now to be Lord of every area of my life:

Lord of my spirit, all of my worship, and my relationship with You;

Lord of my mind, all my thoughts, all my attitudes, and all my behavior;

Lord of my emotions, all my feelings, and all my reactions;

Lord of my will and all my decisions;

Lord of my body and all my physical health;

Lord of my eyes and all that I look upon;

Lord of my ears and all that I listen to;

Lord of my mouth and all that I speak;

Lord of my hands and all that I do;

Lord of my feet and everywhere that I go;

Lord of my sexuality and all its expression;

Lord of my family, my entire home, all my pleasure, and all my relationships;

Lord of my time, all my work, and all my service for You;

Lord of my material goods, all my possessions, all my finances, and all my needs.

Thank You Jesus that Your blood was shed that I might be set free. You and You alone are my Lord and Master. Thank You that my greatest days are yet ahead of me! I'm watching; I'm waiting; and I know I will SEE Your Kingdom come forth in my life, my family, my Church, my community, state, nation, and around the world! Amen!

Chapter 7

"Spiritual Authority, Is it Important?"

"Spiritual Authority, Is it Important?"

I'd like to propose the following questions for your consideration: What is spiritual authority? Do we need spiritual authority? And, who is in spiritual authority? [1]

Let's start here. . .

So Pharaoh asked them, "Can we find anyone like this man, one in whom is the spirit of God?" Genesis 41:38

With these words came the most incredible promotion anyone could ever imagine. Joseph was transported from being a prisoner to the top man in the nation of Egypt, next to the Pharaoh himself. Joseph did more than climb the ladder of success. He bypassed all the rungs and went from the bottom to the top almost overnight. How did he do this? What could possibly prompt an ancient pagan monarch to recognize the spirit of God in a man whom he had never met? Wouldn't it be wonderful if we could rise to the top of our professions in such a quick way? I can remember working on the farm as a teenager, hoping to graduate from pulling weeds by hand to the comfortable seat of the tractor plowing the fields, but it seemed forever before Dad would grant me that promotion; however, it eventually came.

The cold fact is success is never automatic. No matter how hard we try to gain success by doing nothing, it usually doesn't happen. Most people who succeed worked hard to attain their success. To succeed in the Kingdom of God also requires diligence and hard work. It also requires a great deal of faith, for success with God is not measured by the same standards the world uses. We have our set of standards and God has His.

Allow me to share with you a very important principle Joseph possessed in his life that caused his eventual rise to prominence and authority. This principle is taught throughout the Bible and applies to us today. If we hold to this principle, we too will find a greater enhancement of God's blessings. It's just like the time when I was learning to ride a motorcycle as a kid; I only wanted to stay in first gear at the beginning. As a rookie, first gear allowed me to stay at a certain speed, and I liked it. But after a short while, I felt the "need to speed". Knowing that first gear would only permit me to go so fast without burning something up, I applied the second gear. Before long I moved into the highest gears on the bike, taking full advantage of the power available to me.

Now, as I ride my *Yamaha V-star*, I put that baby into the highest gear possible, as quickly as I can, to get to my destination with ease and enjoyment. (And yes, I always wear a helmet.) As you activate this principle I'm about to share with you, I believe you'll find yourself being able to soar higher, breathe longer, take your enemies captive quicker, and be all that God has called you to be – *The Church*.

The Principle

If we want to have spiritual covering in our lives, we must live a life of submission.

Let me explain. In the book of Genesis, take note of the coat of many splendid colors worn by Joseph. It was a gift from his father and is a type, if you will, of the covering we receive from our heavenly Father when we receive the gift of his Son. Jesus covers us in His righteousness, lifting us from sin to Son-ship. Our identities change as a result of His covering.

The idea of "covering" is found throughout the Bible. It symbolizes dependence through submission and without it, we are very vulnerable to Satan and his attacks against us. My bride has a wonderful teaching on spiritual authority, which she equates to an umbrella. As long as we are standing under the umbrella, we are protected from the bad weather. The umbrella of spiritual protection is there to keep the enemy from having an effect upon our lives. The spiritual covering is a protective umbrella of God's mercy and grace. Once we step out from that covering, we are fair game to the enemy.

In the Book of Ruth (a book sometimes referred to as "the romance of redemption") there is an incident where Ruth stealthily lays at the feet of the man who would one day be her husband. The man's name was Boaz and during the barley harvest, which demanded his full attention, he slept in the barn. One night Ruth very quietly sneaked into the barn and proceeded to lie down at his feet. Here is how the Bible describes this event:

Ruth 3:1-11 *One day Naomi her mother-in-law said to her, "My daughter, should I not try to find a home for you, where you will be well provided for? Is not Boaz, with whose servant girls you have been, a kinsman of ours? Tonight he will be winnowing barley on the threshing floor. Wash and perfume yourself, and put on your best clothes. Then go down to the threshing floor, but don't let him know you are there until he has finished eating and drinking. When he lies down, note the place where he is lying. Then go and uncover his feet and lie down. He will tell you what to do." "I will do whatever you say," Ruth answered. So she went down to the threshing floor and did everything her mother-in-law told her to do.*

When Boaz had finished eating and drinking and was in good spirits, he went over to lie down at the far end of the grain pile. Ruth approached quietly, uncovered his feet and lay down. In the middle of the night something startled the man, and he turned and discovered a woman lying at his feet. "Who are you?" he asked.

"I am your servant Ruth," she said. "Spread the corner of your garment over me, since you are a kinsman-redeemer." "The LORD bless you, my daughter," he replied. "This kindness is greater than that which you showed earlier: You have not run after the younger men, whether rich or poor. And now, my daughter, don't be afraid. I will do for you all you ask. All my fellow townsmen know that you are a woman of noble character.

Imagine waking up in the middle of the night and finding a beautiful woman lying at your feet! I'm used to waking up every night to find my beautiful bride Butch lying next to me. But this was not the case with Boaz. He didn't expect her to be there. At first glance one might think of Ruth as being a seductress of some type. However, that was not the case. By asking Baoz to cover her with his garment, Ruth was asking him to marry her. Ruth's former husband had died and afterward Ruth moved to Israel with her mother-in-law, Naomi. It was the custom in Israel for a kinsman to marry a widow in order to preserve the family name and inheritance. Ruth, who had no right to ask for marriage since she was a foreigner, took a great step of faith when she lay at the feet of Boaz.

The truth is, Boaz could have accused her of immorality and made things very difficult for her. Instead, in a spirit of love so similar to that of our Lord's love for us, Boaz left his barley harvest to attend to the more important business of obtaining Ruth as his wife. Ruth's act of submission changed her life forever, and it was for the good.

Let's take a closer look at the story of Joseph, referred to earlier.

In the life of Joseph we see a man who understood submission to those who had authority over him. While he was a boy, Joseph submitted to his father, who in turn loved him very much. Later while in Egypt, Potiphar promoted Joseph because he knew he could trust him. He knew Joseph would never betray the trust he had received, even when approached by Potiphar's wife.

The same was true when the keeper of the prison promoted Joseph. This man was willing to bet his life on Joseph's faithfulness to submit to him. If Joseph ever took advantage of the position he was given and used it as a means of escape, the keeper of the prison could very easily have been executed. It was a cold harsh world back then, but that's what he had to face; and face it he did.

Then came the moment of greatest promotion for Joseph. The Pharaoh himself, the king of Egypt, made Joseph his Prime Minister after Joseph interpreted his dreams. Joseph maintained a life of submission, never abusing the trust placed in him; and through this Joseph became the instrument whereby thousands were spared from a horrible death that would have come their way through famine.

Remember this. . .

To rise to a place of spiritual authority, one must be in submission to the authorities under which God places him or her. In the life of Jesus there was an incident that demonstrates this principle so clearly. It is the story of the healing of the Centurion's servant. Here is how the Bible describes what took place:

Jesus said to him, "I will go and heal him." The centurion replied, "Lord, I do not deserve to have You come under my roof. But just say the word, and my servant will be healed. For I myself am a man under authority, with soldiers under me. I tell this one, 'Go,' and he goes; and that one, 'Come,' and he comes. I say to my servant, 'Do this,' and he does it." When Jesus heard this, He was astonished and said to those following him, "I tell you the truth, I have not found anyone in Israel with such great faith. Matthew 8:7-10

Jesus honored this man's faith and the servant was healed. Notice what the centurion said; *"I am a man under authority, with soldiers under me."* To have authority, one must be under authority. This is a key principle in the Kingdom of God.

It's Not Pointless

In looking at this truth, I believe there are five main areas where God asks us to submit to the authority He has placed over us. Often times when I'm sharing the Word during one of our Sunday Celebrations at Eastgate, I'll have multiple points in my sermon. One time I promised the people that the next sermon I preached would be pointless. Well, this particular teaching has five. It's not pointless.

First, we must submit to the authority of Christ. Paul wrote in 1 Corinthians 11:3, *"The head of every man is Christ."* In this text Paul referred to headship as an ordinance or a tradition that must be observed. Paul stated Christ is the head of the Church and he asked the Church to recognize this fact and live in submission to Christ. *For the husband is head of the wife, as also Christ is head of the Church; and He is the Savior of the Body.* Ephesians 5:23

Second, we are to submit to our parents' authority. Paul said in Ephesians 6:*1, "Children, obey your parents in the Lord, for this is right."* Colossians 3:20 states it like this, *"Children, obey your parents in everything, for this pleases the Lord."* If a child refuses to accept the authority of their parents, then they are actually refusing to accept God's authority, for it is God who gives authority to parents.

Third, God asks us to submit to civil authority. The apostle Paul wrote in Romans 13:1-3, *"Everyone must submit himself to the governing authorities, for there is no authority except that which God has established. The authorities that exist have been established by God. Consequently, he who rebels against the authority is rebelling against what God has instituted, and those who do so will bring judgment on themselves."*

This means we need to obey the laws of our country and includes things like speed limits and other traffic laws. I know this is an issue for most of us, including myself. I usually find myself going faster than the law permits and pretty much have the attitude that I can "get away with it." It's as if, in my subconscious, I believe there are no real consequences to my speeding since I don't get pulled over by law enforcement. But the reality is, when we disobey traffic laws or any other civil law, we are disobeying God, and consequences to this disobedience will come forth one way or the other.

I've found over the years that the blessings come to my life when I live a life of obedience to the Lord and submit to Him in these areas in my life. Let us remind ourselves that there are over 7,000 promises in God's Word; but with each of these promises are premises. If we do our part, then God does His. When I walk in obedience to His premise, then the promise comes forth.

The <u>fourth</u> area of submission is to those for whom we work. Peter wrote in 1 Peter 2:18 *"Slaves, submit yourselves to your masters with all respect, not only to those who are good and considerate, but also to those who are harsh."*

In Biblical days, slavery was practiced in a way that was somewhat different than how we usually think. Back then, some people entered into slavery willingly as a way to pay their debts. Some translations use the word "servant" instead of "slave". The principle Peter sets before us is that we are to submit to those who are over us when it comes to our employment. It does not honor God when we cheat or do not give an honest day's work for the pay we receive.

<u>Fifth</u>, God asks us to submit to spiritual authority. The Book of Hebrews 13:17 states, *"Obey your leaders and submit to their authority. They keep watch over you as men who must give an*

account. Obey them so that their work will be a joy, not a burden, for that would be of no advantage to you."

God has placed pastors, elders, and other leaders in the Church for important reasons. Learn to appreciate and respect them. Do not disregard the things they say and the influence they have in your life. Many have dishonored spiritual leaders by speaking against them or complaining about them (usually when they are not present) and this causes a great deal of spiritual damage in a Church. Submission to spiritual authority is an important key to the success in your life.

Let me add one more. . . (this one is free)

<u>Sixth</u>, all of us need accountability partners we must submit ourselves to. Throughout our ministry, as well as the wonderful friends that God surrounded Butch and I with, He was also kind enough to put some men in my life that I could cry with, rejoice with, be real with, complain to, and be held accountable to; men I consider "bumper pads". The truth is, when you go through the trials of life, you cannot do it on your own. You will need help, which is why we all need "bumper pads."

As I shared in my first book, *"Hey God, Is It Too Much to Ask?"* a dear friend shared this with me a few years ago, and it has saved my life. We need those people in our lives who will hold us accountable and "bump" us back into place when we need it. Those people

174

will be there for us when we feel like our life is heading towards the gutter.

Have you ever been bowling, and could only roll gutter balls? Then someone came up with this handy idea of having bumper pads put into the gutter lanes. They bumped the ball back into place so you could make an impact upon the pins at the end of the lane. That is what each of us need in our lives. These people serve as bumper pads and hold us accountable, and down the straight ways of life so we can make the greatest impact possible. They will be there to cry with us in our times of need. We can depend upon them in our trials.

We all need "bumper pads", and we need them before the crisis arises. We need those people in our lives before we get to the place when we feel like our life is about to end and we cannot move forward any longer.

Another great thing about "bumper pad people" is that they are there to help us see those things in life we cannot necessarily see, and help bump us along the right track. We all have "blind spots", those areas in our lives we cannot see, but they are there. We all have them: things in our lives we cannot see, that we must have someone point out to us. Get a bumper pad and get one quick! Your bumper pads will help you as you wait for your miracle to happen, and they will most likely help keep you from getting yourself into a deeper "pickle", which we often do during these times in our lives.

And by all means, make sure you submit yourself to your "bumper pad." What good will they be to you if this is not a priority in your relationship?

Wrapping It Up

With this knowledge of spiritual authority, we know God has shown us through His Word that it is important for us to be under His authority. But how difficult this task is when spiritual authority begins to spiritually abuse and manipulate us! That is one of the reasons why I've written this book; to be able to be a resource of encouragement to those who have been under an authoritarian, dictator type, power hungry person. There's nothing worse than having those in spiritual authority over us abuse us spiritually and emotionally. One thing we should all be doing. . . praying for those in authority over us. They need it!

Time to Get Real. . .

1. If we want to have a spiritual covering over our lives, we must live a life of _____.

2. What are the five types of authority to which we must submit according to God's Word?

3. What characteristics do you look for in your spiritual authority?

4. Who do you have in your life you consider a spiritual authority?

5. To whom have you submitted yourself for the purpose of training, mentorship and discipling? Who is your Bumper Pad person?

6. In what ways have you found yourself in rebellion to your spiritual authority?

7. Have you ever had a person in spiritual authority over you start out as the kindest, most sensitive person you've known, only to watch them change after submitting to the control of manipulative spirits in their own lives?

Chapter 8

"A Spirit of Manipulation"

"A Spirit of Manipulation"

To put it bluntly, I believe the spirit of manipulation is witchcraft at work.[1] It is a spirit that pretends to be Godly while doing all it can to undermine the true people and the true work of God. Why do Christians abuse one another in the name of the Lord? I am persuaded that most religious exploitation stems from well meaning, though certainly misguided, Church leaders and those in "so called" spiritual authority. Some of that spiritual authority is legit, and some of it is not. Regardless of the purity of their motives, spiritual domination and repression is still injurious; sometimes permanently.

Furthermore, I am convinced that such a style of leadership is a malevolent offspring of a generally accepted misconception of the nature of true Biblical leadership. Leaders in the Church, according to the New Testament especially as taught and exemplified by Christ, are instructed to lead from a lowly posture of servitude and love; not from some lofty pedestal of entitlement, usurped authority, and privilege we see far too often in the Church mindset of today's culture.

So, where does it say: "Manipulation is Witchcraft" in the Bible? It's got to be there somewhere; right? Well, believe it or not I've been looking for it and I can't seem to find it. Yet, a lot of people tend to quote this religiously. The fact is scripture doesn't specifically say this, but it's obviously sinful. Manipulation isn't actually mentioned as a form of witchcraft. But it is a sin in which people manipulate situations or others, seeking 'glory' for themselves, rather than being motivated to show God's Glory to others.

God defines witchcraft as sorcery, fortune telling, dream interpretation, idol worship, etc., which He says is forbidden . . . Exodus 22:18 states death is the punishment for witchcraft. All God's commands are given to protect us, not to force us to follow the Leader - God gave us free will.

My friend Don Flannery's definition of witchcraft is: "Attempting to control events or outcomes through bending or marshaling natural or spiritual forces to do your will."

Witchcraft exposes people to the 'powers of darkness', which can defeat them by resulting in spiritual death. Ephesians 6:10-12 states: *"Be strong in the Lord and in His mighty power. Put on the full armor of God so that you can take your stand against the devil's schemes. For our struggle is not against flesh and blood, but against the rulers, against the authorities, against the powers of this dark world and against the spiritual forces of evil in the heavenly realms."*

I have found that the Bible condemns witchcraft about 20 times. And in regards to the question, "Where is manipulation as witchcraft?" found in the Bible, the closest verses I can find are the following. . .

You were nothing more than a prostitute using your magical charms and witchcraft to attract and trap nations. Nahum 3: 4

For some time a man named Simon had lived in the city of Samaria and had amazed the people. He practiced witchcraft and claimed to be somebody great. Everyone, rich and poor, crowded around him. They said, "This man is the power of God called `The Great Power.' " For a long time, Simon had used witchcraft to amaze the people, and they kept crowding around him. Acts 8: 9-11

And, then . . . God "stepped in" — vs. 12 & 13 - *But when they believed what Philip was saying about God's Kingdom and about the name of Jesus Christ, they were all baptized. Even Simon believed and was baptized. He stayed close to Philip, because he marveled at all the miracles and wonders.*

The modern Church mindset, unlike the apostolic Church we find in the New Testament, seems to insist on venerating its leaders — or perhaps, more accurately, leaders venerate themselves — to exalted offices. Ministers, assuming elitist roles, regularly corrupt terms like "the anointing," "the calling," and "authority" to infer that their bureaucratic offices and spiritual gifting's are exclusive Biblical endowments and that they, because of some special empowerment, are somehow exceptional. If one challenges this, they are often quoted the scripture, *"Touch not the hand of God's anointed"* or other such scriptures taken out of context.

In efforts to underscore this clerical distinction that ministers have a higher calling, ministers have, over the centuries, adopted visible symbolic accouterments to set themselves apart and further demarcate their status. These may include vestments, collars, stoles, chasubles, surplices, and even in modern times, designer Armani suits, Versace neckties, and fancy loafers. The term we used to use on the Reservation when growing up was, "Don't you look all fancy-dancy!?"

I can remember at one time thinking that if I didn't wear a suit and tie when I preached, people wouldn't take me seriously; thus, I wore a suit and tie every time I preached. I literally thought it would enhance my authority and that people would "have" to listen to me if I looked the part. I was unknowingly practicing manipulation by the motive behind choosing the clothes I wore.

To further reinforce their assumed privileged status and assumed license, clerics, despite Christ's clear instruction to the contrary, commonly employ exaggerated, self-inflated, hierarchal titles as "Reverend," "Bishop," "Sr. Pastor," "Doctor," "Elder," "Prophet," even "Apostle" or sometimes, "First Lady." While there is nothing wrong with using such terms to identify one's function or ministry, using them as titles of *special rank* could, nonetheless, seem clearly prohibited.

Famous Movie Quote:

1975 movie MONTY PYTHON AND THE HOLY GRAIL[2]

King Arthur: *"I am your king."*

Woman: *"Well I didn't vote for you."*

King Arthur: *"You don't vote for kings."*

Woman: *"Well how'd you become king then?"*

[Angelic music plays. . .]

King Arthur: *"The Lady of the Lake, her arm clad in the purest shimmering samite held aloft Excalibur from the bosom of the water, signifying by divine providence that I, Arthur, was to carry Excalibur. THAT is why I am your king."*

[interrupting]

Dennis: *"Listen, strange women lyin' in ponds distributin' swords is no basis for a system of government. Supreme executive power derives from a mandate from the masses, not from some farcical aquatic ceremony."*

Then Jesus spoke to the multitudes and to His disciples, saying: "The scribes and the Pharisees sit in Moses' seat. Therefore whatever they tell you to observe, that observe and do, but do not do according to their works; for they say, and do not do. For they bind heavy burdens, hard to bear, and lay them on men's shoulders; but they themselves will not move them with one of their fingers. But all their works they do to be seen by men. They make their phylacteries broad and enlarge the borders of their garments. They love the best places at feasts, the best seats in the synagogues, greetings in the marketplaces, and to be called by men, 'Rabbi, Rabbi.' But you, do not be called 'Rabbi'; for One is your Teacher, the Christ, and you are all brethren. Do not call anyone on earth your father; for One is your Father, He who is in heaven. And do not be called teachers; for One is your Teacher, the Christ. But he who is greatest among you shall be your servant." Matthew 23:1-11 (NKJV)

I'm all for giving honor to those who have earned honor and their titled position by referring to them as such. But these self-proclaimed titles and exaggerated references do nothing but enhance the whole perception of misguided leaders who manipulate the Church. I am now at the point in my life I could care less if you call me Pastor Dale, Pastor Dave, PD, Apostle, P-didee or whatever you like. (Just don't call me late for tacos!)

In this text, you'll read about the greatness of serving. Matthew 20:20-28 (NKJV) *Then the mother of Zebedee's sons came to Him with her sons, kneeling down and asking something from Him. And He said to her, "What do you wish?" She said to Him, "Grant that these two sons of mine may sit, one on Your right hand and the other on the left, in Your kingdom." But Jesus answered and said, "You do not know what you ask. Are you able to drink the cup that I am about to drink, and be baptized with the baptism that I am baptized with?" They said to Him, "We are able."*

So He said to them, "You will indeed drink My cup, and be baptized with the baptism that I am baptized with; but to sit on My right hand and on My left is not Mine to give, but it is for those for whom it is prepared by My Father."

And when the ten heard it, they were greatly displeased with the two brothers. But Jesus called them to Himself and said, "You know that the rulers of the Gentiles lord it over them, and those who are great exercise authority over them. Yet it shall not be so among you; but whoever desires to become great among you, let him be your servant. And whoever desires to be first among you, let him be your slave - just as the Son of Man did not come to be served, but to serve, and to give His life a ransom for many."

I love this text in Mark 10:42-45 (NKJV). *But Jesus called them to Himself and said to them, "You know that those who are considered rulers over the Gentiles lord it over them, and their great ones exercise authority over them. Yet it shall not be so among you; but whoever desires to become great among you shall be your servant. And whoever of you desires to be first shall be slave of all. For even the Son of Man did not come to be served, but to serve, and to give His life a ransom for many."*

Now, if that isn't enough scripture for you, check out this disagreement the disciples are having about greatness, to which Jesus pretty much puts them in order. *Now there was also a dispute among them, as to which of them should be considered the greatest. And He said to them, "The kings of the Gentiles exercise lordship over them, and those who exercise authority over them are called 'benefactors.' But not so among you; on the contrary, he who is greatest among you, let him be as the younger, and he who governs as he who serves. For who is greater, he who sits at the table, or he who serves? Is it not he who sits at the table? Yet I am among you as the One who serves."* Luke 22:24-27 (NKJV)

Do you want more Biblical proof?

Okay, then check out John 13:14-17 (NKJV). *If I then, your Lord and Teacher, have washed your feet, you also ought to wash one another's feet. For I have given you an example, that you should do as I have done to you. Most assuredly, I say to you, a servant is not greater than his master; nor is he who is sent greater than he who sent him. If you know these things, blessed are you if you do them.*

Let's go a bit deeper; I hope you can swim

In the book of Ezra, the people of God had decided it was time for a change. It was time to once again establish the Kingdom of God in the land. The people of God had started to rebuild the temple.

When the enemies of Judah and Benjamin heard that the exiles were building a temple for the Lord, the God of Israel, they came to Zerubbabel and to the heads of the families and said, "Let us help you build because, like you, we seek your God and have been sacrificing to him since the time of Esarhaddon king of Assyria, who brought us here." But Zerubbabel, Jeshua and the rest of the heads of the families of Israel answered, "You have no part with us in building a temple to our God. We alone will build it for the Lord, the God of Israel, as King Cyrus, the king of Persia, commanded us." Ezra 4:1-3 NIV

In reading this, we can begin to see the spirit of manipulation will first pretend it belongs in the Church. The spirit of manipulation will pretend it is holy and doing the work of God. The spirit of manipulation will masquerade as a Christian. The leaders discerned the false motives of their hearts. They rejected the spirit of manipulation. The leaders chose to obey God and not submit to the manipulative spirits.

Then the peoples around them set out to discourage the people of Judah and make them afraid to go on building. They hired counselors to work against them and frustrate their plans during the entire reign of Cyrus king of Persia and down to the reign of Darius king of Persia. At the beginning of the reign of Xerxes, they lodged an accusation against the people of Judah and Jerusalem. And in the days of Artaxerxes king of Persia, Bishlam, Mithredath, Tabeel and the rest of his associates wrote a letter to Artaxerxes. The letter was written in Aramaic script and in the Aramaic language. Rehum the commanding officer and Shimshai the secretary wrote a letter against Jerusalem to Artaxerxes the king. Ezra 4:4-8 (NIV)

Now the spirit of manipulation began to see who in the Church would be willing to listen to murmuring and complaining. They began to whisper in the Church about the character of the leaders. They began to speak about their plans, which they believed were better. They began to sow seeds of disunity because the spirit of manipulation was not in control. Eventually the spirit of manipulation found access to the king and swayed the opinion of the king against the Church. How many times have we seen this play itself out in the modern day Church culture? I'm sorry to say too many times.

The whispers of Church members against the leadership will always be detrimental in its very nature. There is a reason God tells us in His Word to refrain from gossip and murmuring. There is a reason this type of behavior and speech will be destructive to the core of who the Church is and is supposed to be.

Do you recall what sound sheep make? The sound is usually, "Baaaaaaaa." However, the sheep in the Church that have a tendency to always complain, murmur, gossip, etc. are heard to say, "Meeeeeeee." We're not supposed to be saying "Meeeeee"; we are supposed to be saying, "Baaaaaaaa." But for those folks in the Church who are self-focused, it's all about, "Meeeeeeee." Sorry, but it is not supposed to be about <u>you</u>. It is supposed to be about <u>others</u>!

Feel like singing?

I'm reminded of the children's song we use to sing in our Church on the Reservation when growing up. "JOY" [3]. The lyrics are as follows. . .

Jesus and others then you; What a wonderful way to spell joy!
Jesus and others then you; In the life of each girl and each boy.
J is for Jesus, for He has first place;
O is for others we meet face to face.
Y is for you in whatever you do;
Put yourself third and spell joy.

Let's go on. *As soon as the copy of the letter of King Artaxerxes was read to Rehum and Shimshai the secretary and their associates, they went immediately to the Jews in Jerusalem and compelled them by force to stop. Thus the work on the house of God in Jerusalem came to a standstill until the second year of the reign of Darius king of Persia.* Ezra 4:23-24 (NIV)

The spirit of manipulation seemed successful at halting the work of God. Now the people of God needed some supernatural encouragement. One thing to keep in mind when dealing with manipulative people . . . a prophetic Godly word always carries more power than the spirit of manipulation. In fact, **one Word**

from the Lord can bring down a thousand words spoken by the enemy!

Now Haggai the prophet and Zechariah the prophet, a descendant of Iddo, prophesied to the Jews in Judah and Jerusalem in the name of the God of Israel, who was over them. Then Zerubbabel son of Shealtiel and Jeshua son of Jozadak set to work to rebuild the house of God in Jerusalem. And the prophets of God were with them, helping them. Ezra 5:1-2 (NIV)

The prophets of God will serve alongside the people of God to see God's purposes fulfilled. The beautiful thing is, as we walk in obedience to God's Word, His purposes will always be fulfilled, in His timing and His ways. He's more than willing and able to do His part; He's just waiting on us, the Church, to do ours. He's waiting for us to stop being manipulated and do what He's called and designed for us to do, before time ever began.

In looking at this scripture, we see that eventually the prophets and the people of God revealed the truth to the king. The king decreed that the people of God could continue to rebuild the temple of God.

Then, because of the decree King Darius had sent, Tattenai, governor of Trans-Euphrates, and Shethar-Bozenai and their associates carried it out with diligence. So the elders of the Jews continued to build and prosper under the preaching of Haggai the prophet and Zechariah, a descendant of Iddo. They finished building the temple according to the command of the God of Israel and the decrees of Cyrus, Darius and Artaxerxes, kings of Persia. The temple was completed on the third day of the month Adar, in the sixth year of the reign of King Darius. Then the people of Israel—the priests, the Levites and the rest of the exiles— celebrated the dedication of the house of God with joy. For the dedication of this house of God they offered a hundred bulls, two hundred rams, four hundred male lambs and, as a sin offering for all Israel, twelve male goats, one for each of the tribes of Israel. And they installed the priests in their divisions and the Levites in their groups for the service of God at Jerusalem, according to what is written in the Book of Moses. Ezra 6:13-18 (NIV)

The people of God prospered because the prophets and their leaders were not afraid to confront the spirit of manipulation; they stood up and decided they would no longer allow themselves to be manipulated. Because they showed courage, the people were able to once again restore the Kingdom of God in their land. Once again the people of God were obeying the Word of God.

This brings to mind a conversation of courage between the Cowardly Lion and Dorothy in the famous movie THE WIZARD OF OZ.

Famous Movie Quote:

1939 Movie THE WIZARD OF OZ [3]

Cowardly Lion: *"Courage! What makes a king out of a slave? Courage! What makes the flag on the mast to wave? Courage!*

What makes the elephant charge his tusk in the misty mist, or the dusky dusk? What makes the muskrat guard his musk? Courage! What makes the sphinx the seventh wonder? Courage! What makes the dawn come up like thunder? Courage! What makes the Hottentot so hot? What puts the "ape" in apricot? What have they got that I ain't got?"

Dorothy, Scarecrow, Tin Woodsman: *"Courage!"*

Cowardly Lion: *"You can say that again! Huh?"*

If we as the body of Christ would stand up and stop being manipulated, I believe we would see our lives and the lives of those around us begin to be restored. Then, when the hearts of the Church family are restored, we'll begin to see the heart of a nation restored. If we want to see our nation restored to its Godly heritage and our cities transformed, we will have to fight against the spirit of manipulation that finds itself at home pretending to be a part of the Church.

Check this out. . .

When someone "has a controlling, manipulative spirit," it doesn't necessarily mean they have a demon instigating the control. There are some people who think that a person who is living the life of one who abuses and manipulates is always possessed. This is not true. It can simply mean they are yielding to their own human desire to be in control. (Though there may be some who are possessed.)

The controlling spirit likely stems from our tendency toward the "pride of life" John mentions in 1 John 2:16 (NKJV). *For all that is in the world—the lust of the flesh, the lust of the eyes, and the pride of life—is not of the Father but is of the world.*

The reason for this is because it involves trying to get others to do our will. It doesn't have to be limited to just people. In our pride, we may even try to get God to do our will through selfish or controlling prayers.

The controlling spirit typically uses manipulation to accomplish its purposes. Merriam-Webster Dictionary defines manipulation as: "to control or play upon by artful, unfair, or insidious means, especially to one's own advantage; to change by artful or unfair means so as to serve one's purpose." [5] As we can see by that definition, manipulation is self-centered and has nothing to do with love. You, *The Church*, however, should have everything to do with love!

Time to Get Real...

1. What two words does Jesus use to describe a great leader according to Mark 10:42-45?

2. What description of the Pharisees' works does Jesus give in Matthew 23:1-11? Are we supposed to follow their example?

3. Have you experienced clergy members or leaders of Christian organizations that have given you the impression they are more spiritual than you? How did that make you feel?

4. Have you had someone tell you, "God told me this...?" How did that make you feel and what was your response to them?

Did you just "go along with it" or did you question their validity?

Chapter 9

"A Spirit of Jezebel"

"A Spirit of Jezebel"

*M*uch has been written about a Spirit of Jezebel in the past. It seems that to be a preacher you must minister on this spirit at least once in your ministry. Even I have a series of lessons I have shared and taught on many occasions. When we clergy face someone who is unruly, disobedient, or has an "issue", it is easy to pin the Spirit of Jezebel label on him or her. The fact is, it is wrong. We might think our intentions are to help them, but in reality we are trying to manipulate.

We do need to recognize there is a Spirit of Jezebel that is alive and well.[1] This spirit can and will control you, if you allow it. We, the Church, need to stand up against this spirit with all of the authority given to us by God and walk in the reality of Truth that God is more powerful than this spirit. **We can walk in freedom from it!**

In 1 and 2 Kings we find that Jezebel was a powerful, wicked queen, and wife of a passive king called Ahab. She was a false prophetess who worshiped the false god, Baal. Baal was the god of prosperity, god of the harvests, god of fertility, and god of sex. Child sacrifices were common. In the end, she was killed by several eunuchs at the order of commander Jehu.

Jezebel was a witch, and her spirit of witchcraft is still in operation today in and outside the Church. It will take both a Jehu and the cooperation of the injured victims (spiritual eunuchs) to kill her again.

You can read up on this spirit in the myriad of writings and teachings on the Internet that have come out in past years. Thus, I won't take the time or space to give you all the details. But allow me to share with you fifteen of the behaviors you might see in a person who is operating under the influence of the Spirit of Jezebel.[2] I realize these are generalizations, but I've found them to be pretty right on when dealing with this spirit.

15 Spirit of Jezebel Behavioral Patterns

1. They gain power by destroying others. It is like an adrenalin rush when they "win" over someone. They manage to obtain positions of authority and are difficult to displace once there. Thus you must be very careful whom you place in these positions, remembering that it's always easier to get them in than it is to get them out. It is always easier to go into debt than to get out of debt. It is easier to make a mess than it is to clean up a mess. A person who operates under the influence of Jezebel will be much more difficult

to get out. The difficult thing is that they are extremely well adapted to persuading others and making themselves *look* good. Thus, great discernment is needed on your part.

2. They are controlling, manipulative and bossy. Most of the time you'll not experience this at the beginning of their relationship with you, for they will be trying to win you over. After the "honeymoon" is over, they will be very bossy, keeping you hopping from one project to another. They will try to control you in every way possible. They come on slowly, but will build in their intensity as you continue your relationship.

3. They can either be war-like in their personalities, so that they are intimidating, or so sweet, perfect, timid, and sneaky that they are able to fool and recruit others to join them. Sometimes they can be very charming and charismatic. I hate to admit I have been fooled in the past by more than one person who has operated in this way. I am thankful I have a discerning bride, Butch, who helps keep me out of trouble in this area. I have found that a tear down the cheek or a sad story can easily persuade me; but she's got a knack for spotting those under the influence of the Spirit of Jezebel a mile away.

4. They tend to be very critical of others, and sometimes vicious, to the point of being emotionally bloodthirsty. Sometimes this critical spirit will manifest itself right in the face of others, but most of the time it's behind their back. Those under the influence of the Spirit of Jezebel will speak critically of someone (usually under the guise of how they can help him or her). Often saying, "This is how

we s..ould be praying for them;" they will mask the critical opinions of others in a guise of prayer and concern, all the while cutting them to the quick.

5. They are never wrong. Sure, they may admit to being wrong in certain cases, but that's only to stay on your good side and make you think they're humble. However, they continue to maintain their attitude of being right as soon as they leave your presence. They tend to have the thought that everything they do is right and their opinions are right no matter what the circumstances. And if you come against their opinions and truths, watch out - they will cunningly devise a secret plan to make you look bad in the eyes of others.

6. They recruit others to join with them in their opinions of others. They act to persuade recruits and do not give up this activity until they have won over the recruits. If the potential recruits do not cooperate and buy into things, this angers them. They will go out of their way to get people on their side and will include them in their discussions when talking to others. Those under the influence of the Spirit of Jezebel will say things like, "There are a lot of people who are dissatisfied with. . ." I've learned that when I confront them about who these people are, they usually respond with "that's confidential;" or they can't name anyone because that "just wouldn't be right" and they skirt the issue.

Here comes an Arrrggghhhhh!

7. <u>Everything</u> is confidential. When you confront those under the influence of the Spirit of Jezebel with details about their concerns or ask about the people whom they say are upset, the answer is always *"confidential!"* Arrrggghhhhh! It's an easy scapegoat (an easy way to get out of something) when they say this; but it is used all the time, and it drives me bananas!

8. They are narcissistic and play the part of the victim. While often they tend to be oversensitive themselves, they have no concern for the feelings of others. Those influenced by a spirit of Jezebel are not sympathetic to their victims, and tend to play the role of victim themselves in order to gain sympathy. This way the real victim is left stranded and opposed by others if they should ask for help. Being the center of attention really pleases them. It always amazes me how they can turn a situation around in which they created harm, but they become the victim. What a sneaky and manipulative art! They want others to feel sorry for them when they are the ones who caused the hurt in the first place!

They have a complete lack of remorse after hurting someone. In fact, those under the influence of the Spirit of Jezebel have a way of justifying the harm they caused and becoming the victims themselves. They will give you the impression (to your face) that they are sorry for hurting you; but behind your back, you're fresh bait.

9. They lie, and sadly, they believe their own lie. Avoiding the truth, or intentionally acting to withhold truth is part of this. A false picture is usually presented to others. Those under the influence of the Spirit of Jezebel will look you in the eye and say one thing and then leave the room and say something else. They will hear what they want to hear and not necessarily what you are actually saying. It grieves my heart that many of them actually believe their own lies to the point they think these lies are truths, and nothing will persuade them otherwise.

A friend of mine in the Philippines says it this way, "I'm responsible for what I say, not for what you hear." That is the hard part though. Although we do our best to say the right thing and speak in truth, they often hear only what they want to hear and then spread what they "heard" as a lie.

10. They are usually impulsive, failing to plan ahead. Because of this, they can live a very chaotic life. Everything seems to be urgent and must be done now. They are always busy with doing "Kingdom-of-God work" but never seem to actually get it done. So, because they are impulsive and fail to plan ahead, they just "go for it". But in the process of going for it, they leave a wake of chaos and confusion in their path.

11. They are consistently irresponsible. Deadlines are missed on a regular basis. But these missed deadlines usually always have a Godly justification behind them. When asked to accomplish something, if it's not going to better their life or make them look good

in some way, they usually put it off until they "have" to do it. Then those under the influence of the Spirit of Jezebel can always find something incredibly important that had to be done first to absolve themselves of their tardiness.

I once worked with an individual who constantly blamed his/her family for not completing their assignments. They would always come to me and say something like, "Pastor, my family is in great need of such and such right now, and therefore I'm not going to be able to accomplish what you've asked me to do." What could I say? For Pete's sake, I was the one who told them to make sure their family is always first place in their lives outside of their walk with God. But they would use it against me. Manipulation. Is your family a priority? Absolutely. But don't use that as an excuse to get out of doing something. You have a responsibility to carry out your job assignments given to you. As Larry the Cable guy would say, "*Git-r-done.*"

12. They are irritable, aggressive (either openly or subtly), and quick tempered. When confronted, they can be very disruptive in a conversation. They'll take a nice atmosphere where people are enjoying each other and then turn it into an atmosphere where suddenly everyone is walking on eggshells. Have you ever walked on eggshells before? Not an easy thing to do, believe me.

13. They show passive-aggressive behaviors. They will argue with you, but they'll do it with scripture. They will confront with love in front of others but have a hidden motive of causing you

harm. They are aggressive when confronting you, but they go about it in a very passive way. Passive-aggressive behavior is dealing with expectations in interpersonal or occupational situations in an obstructionist or hostile manner. It indicates aggression, or, in more general terms, expressing aggression in non-assertive (i.e. passive or indirect) ways. It can be seen in some cases as a personality trait or disorder marked by a pervasive pattern of negative attitudes and passive, usually disavowed, resistance in interpersonal or occupational situations.

With many people who deal with this, passive-aggressive behavior can manifest itself as learned helplessness, procrastination, hostility masquerading as jokes, stubbornness, resentment, sullenness, or deliberate/repeated failure to accomplish requested tasks for which one is (often explicitly) responsible. At first, they falsely accuse you behind your back in very subtle and passive ways, and then later will make it public once they have enough people to support their claims.

14. They fail to conform to social norms. Those under the influence of the Spirit of Jezebel are usually "outsiders" or non-conformists and have their own way of doing things. They do not always like being around a crowd of people that "get along with each other". They will look upon those as a threat to them, thus not wanting to be a participant within the function of the group.

15. They refuse to get help. When confronted by someone to get help, which is usually by someone in their life like a pastor or

spiritual leader, they will go through the motions of saying they want help and might actually even go to get help; but they have no desire to actually receive help or change. They will go only to please you and make you think they're doing what you've asked, all along playing the game of manipulating you. The fact is, psychological counseling will not help, since they deny that they are influenced and controlled by the spirit of Jezebel.

Time to Get Real. . .

1. What are some of the behaviors exhibited by someone influenced by a Spirit of Jezebel?
2. Have you ever met a person who operates in a Spirit of Jezebel either knowingly or unknowingly?
3. Without naming names, what were your initial thoughts about this person before you started to realize that they were manipulating you?
4. What were the signs this person was trying to manipulate you?
5. Have you ever confronted a person operating under the influence of this spirit? Would you do it again? Why or why not?
6. Have you ever operated in this mode? Out of the 15 traits, which ones are you guilty of?
7. If you've been guilty in the past of operating in this mode, how did you stop?

Chapter 10

"The TRUE Manipulator"

"The TRUE Manipulator"

*A*s my friend Ford Taylor says, "When it all boils down, we only have one enemy, and it's not each other. It's the devil." Yes, he uses all of us as puppets in his manipulative ways to get us to manipulate others, but the true source of all manipulation comes from the devil himself. He is the source of all evil and will do everything he can to manipulate us into turning our backs on God and keeping us, *The Church*, from making an impact in the world in which we live.

There is nothing good about the devil, not one thing. This reminds me of the quote from the movie RAIDERS OF THE LOST ARK. . .

Famous Movie Quote:

1981 Movie RAIDERS OF THE LOST ARK[1]

Indiana: *"Here, take this."* [hands Marion a torch]

Indiana: *"Wave it at anything that slithers."*

Marion: *"The whole place is slitherin'!"*

So, let's look at this age-old enemy called Satan as we learn a little about the true enemy who manipulates us for his own gain.

THE DEFINITION OF SATAN

The definition of Satan or Devil or Lucifer literally means, an adversary, antagonist, or accuser, prosecutor and persecutor, or one who distresses or oppresses. In Zechariah 3:1-2 the title adversary is given. (NKJV) *Then he showed me Joshua the high priest standing before the Angel of the LORD, and Satan standing at his right hand to oppose him. And the LORD said to Satan, "The LORD rebuke you, Satan! The LORD who has chosen Jerusalem rebuke you! Is this not a brand plucked from the fire?"* We find it to mean, destroyer, one to cause demise, one who devours manipulates and demolishes.

THE PURPOSE OF SATAN

His purpose is to dissolve and diminish the faith of God's children, to decapitate their trust and to cause their hope to die. He has distinct characteristics that indicate determination to delete those who love God, and he will manipulate everyone in his path to make this happen.

THE WILL OF SATAN

Satan's "will" for your life – <u>Death</u>. The death of your physical life, the death of your marriage, the death of your dreams, the death of your finances, etc.

God's "will" for your life – <u>Life</u>. Physical, emotional, spiritual, financial and every other "al" there is!

THE JOB DESCRIPTION OF SATAN

Satan's job description indicates one who is out to cause chaos and confusion through forms of manipulation, control, and abuse. So when adversity intrudes in your life, it is necessary for you to understand; Satan will attack those who love the Lord, simply because he already owns those who refuse to acknowledge God. Why go after what you already own? He'll spend a great deal of time attempting to manipulate you as a believer in Christ more than one who does not know Him.

THE ORIGIN OF SATAN

Who is the devil and where does he come from? As you study the Bible you will observe that nowhere in the Bible is there any attempt to *prove* the existence of the devil. It is assumed that there is an actual personality known as Satan. To learn something of the origin of this creature of manipulation we need to look at. . . Ezekiel 28:12-19

NOTE: This passage is primarily a reference to the King of Tyre. But the verses obviously go beyond the man to the motivating force and personality who was compelling him in his opposition to God. The prophet saw the work and activity of Satan, who the King of Tyre was emulating in so many ways.

#1: Satan is A Created Being

(Ezekiel 28:12-14) We are taught in this passage that the devil is a created being. Verse 14 teaches he was created as an anointed cherub. A cherub in the Word of God seems to be the *highest order of angelic beings in heaven.*

12 "Son of man, take up a lamentation for the king of Tyre, and say to him, 'Thus says the Lord God: "You were the seal of perfection, Full of wisdom and perfect in beauty.

13 You were in Eden, the garden of God; Every precious stone was your covering: The sardius, topaz, and diamond, Beryl, onyx, and jasper, Sapphire, turquoise, and emerald with Gold. The workmanship of your timbrels and pipes was prepared for you on the day you were created.

14 "You were the anointed cherub who covers; I established you; You were on the holy mountain of God; You walked back and forth in the midst of fiery stones.

Look at verse 14 again, "an anointed cherub that covers. . ." The word "covers" could be translated "that guards." This anointed cherub was set-aside for the specific purpose of guarding access to the throne of God.

#2: Satan is A Corrupted Being (Ezekiel 28:15)

15 You were perfect in your ways from the day you were created, Till iniquity was found in you.

(Verse 15) — The devil became a corrupted being. One of the age-old questions of theology is presented here. What is the origin of evil? We know that Satan tempted Adam and Eve. Who tempted Satan? We can discover what his sin was, but we are left to conjecture where the desire came from. From these verses and from the passage in Isaiah 14:9, we can discern that the reason for Lucifer's fall was pride.

The Bible says, "*Pride goeth before destruction and an haughty spirit before a fall.*" The moment we allow pride to come into our heart, God says we are headed for a fall!

Luke 10:18 makes mention of this when Jesus says, "*I beheld Satan fall as lightning from heaven.*" We are given indication in other verses in Revelation 12, Jude 6, and 2 Peter 2:4 that the devil carried with him a third of the angels of heaven in his fall. They make up a vast horde of demons (evil spirits) that do the devil's bidding.

#3: Satan is A Condemned Being

God has pronounced His condemnation upon the devil and declared that eventually he will be cast into hell. The devil has retained some authority and power. Jesus said in John 12:31, *"that the devil is the prince of this world."* Again in Ephesians 2:2 Paul tells us that,*"the devil is the prince of the power of the air."* But in Genesis 3:15 we have the first gospel message preached to man and it pronounces condemnation on the devil, *"And I will put enmity between you and the woman, and between your seed and her Seed; He shall bruise your head, and you shall bruise His heel."*

(Ezekiel 28:16-19)

16 "By the abundance of your trading you became filled with violence within, And you sinned; Therefore I cast you as a profane thing out of the mountain of God; And I destroyed you, O covering cherub, from the midst of the fiery stones.

17 Your heart was lifted up because of your beauty; you corrupted your wisdom for the sake of your splendor; I cast you to the ground, I laid you before kings that they might gaze at you.

18 You defiled your sanctuaries by the multitude of your iniquities, by the iniquity of your trading; Therefore I brought fire from your midst; it devoured you, and I turned you to ashes upon the earth in the sight of all who saw you.

19 All who knew you among the peoples are astonished at you; you have become a horror, and shall be no more forever."

How Does Satan Operate?

It is very important for us to understand how the devil operates as he manipulates us. We are warned in 1 Peter 5:8. Notice from the Bible how the devil would devour us. *Be sober, be vigilant; because your adversary the devil walks about like a roaring lion, seeking whom he may <u>devour</u>.*

First of all, <u>Mentally</u>

The devil wants your mind and will do everything he can to manipulate your thought processes. <u>Keep in mind he cannot nor will he ever be able to read your mind.</u> But he seeks to destroy the minds of men through lies. God confronts the mind of man with truth. In John 17:17 the Bible says, *"Thy word is truth."* **If the promises and truths of God's word can be absorbed in your soul, your life will be different; you will never again be the same.**

In John 8:44 the Bible tells us that the devil is a liar from the beginning. (NKJV) *You are of your father the devil, and the desires of your father you want to do. He was a murderer from the beginning, and does not stand in the truth, because there is no truth in him. When he speaks a lie, he speaks from his own resources, for he is a liar and the father of it.* There is no truth in him; every time he speaks, he speaks a lie, for he is a liar and the father of lies and the chief manipulator. The ultimate source of all untruth is the devil. If the devil can cause you to believe his lies, he has moved you closer to wrecking your life.

Second, <u>Morally</u>

The devil attacks us morally. He wants our heart as well as our mind. He wants us to love the things we ought to hate and hate the things we ought to love. The heart of man was made to love the Lord Jesus. God made us that way! That is why children instinctively love Jesus. But the devil seeks to replace that love with the love of sin. He does it by making sin attractive and alluring. He uses the pleasures of sin to enslave us morally. Look at the more obvious examples in this world and how they are glorified: drinking, sex, gambling, murder. If the devil can get us to love sin, he gains a foothold in our heart. Before long we are morally enslaved through his traps of manipulation.

And then thirdly, <u>Motivationally</u>

The devil wants to take our will. In 2 Timothy 2:26 Paul talks about the snare of the devil and being taken captive by him at his will. We fail to understand that the devil has a will for our lives just as God does. His purpose is to trap us and bring us into absolute subjection to his will. All sin is addictive. All sin is habit forming. We can see this in any sin you care to name: alcohol, drugs, lying, gossip, the love of money. All of these will possess you if Satan takes over your will.

My daughter Linzi has written a number of poems that have been published over the years. Each of her poems minister to the hearts of individuals at certain times in their lives. This particular poem encouraged me during a season of battle and gave me the desire to continue moving forward. I hope it does the same for you.

The Strength to Overcome
By Linzi LaRai Campfield [2]

Did You think of me before the stars were formed?
Did you know me before you breathed life into dust?
I long to be free from the things that bind me; the chains that grip
me so tight.
So what can I do to be rid of these thoughts? To be rid of the sin
that so easily entraps?
What can I do to be free?
Time & time again I have failed,
Yet even as I have slipped out of the light of hopeful freedom,
And into the darkness again,
Your unconditional love draws me close
And beckons my restless heart to peace.
My God, The God, who created the structure of the universe,
Who knew time before time began
And who was captivated with me before I was born,
Has the power to demolish strongholds and death

And to bring me freedom from my sin.

He loves me with an unquenchable love

And He will give me the strength to overcome.

Have you ever wanted something so badly you'd do anything to have it? How strong is your desire level to overcome? This passion for truth comes to my mind when watching the movie The Matrix, with Neo's desire for the true reality of his life.

Famous Movie Quote:

1999 Movie THE MATRIX [3]

Trinity: *"I know why you're here, Neo. I know what you've been doing. . . why you hardly sleep, why you live alone, and why night after night, you sit by your computer. You're looking for him. I know because I was once looking for the same thing. And when he found me, he told me I wasn't really looking for him. I was looking for an answer. It's the question that drives us, Neo. It's the question that brought you here. You know the question, just as I did."*

Neo: *"What is the Matrix?"*

Trinity: *"The answer is out there, Neo, and it's looking for you, and it will find you if you want it to."*

Question: Is all of the manipulation I deal with Satan's fault?

The short answer. No. There is a myth out there that Satan is the source of all our problems. If you are like most people, you think all of your temptations, all of your evil thoughts, and all of those forms of manipulation that come your way come from Satan. Many of them do, and many of them don't.

Most of us remember the comedian, Flip Wilson, who used to say, *"The devil made me do it!"* And we think the devil makes us do everything bad. That is wrong, too. We have a free will. The devil can offer you all the temptations in the world by manipulating you day and night and that is all they are – temptations. He cannot make you accept them. And he will make those temptations look almost too good to pass up, but the key word is "almost." Thankfully, we have great strength that will enable us to turn down his gift.

James 4:7 tells us that we can resist the devil, *"So obey God. Stand up to the devil. He will run away from you."* So, even though Satan can influence us, we do have the strength to resist him. That strength is found in Christ Jesus. Philippians 4:13 states, *"I can do everything by the power of Christ, who gives me strength."*

4:13

Years ago I set the alarm on my cell phone to ring at 4:13 p.m. I preached a message during one of our celebration services and encouraged the entire Church family to do the same. Then, every day when the alarm would ring they would remember the verse Philippians 4:13, and be encouraged that God was there to help them through all they dealt with in their lives.

Do you know what's really cool right now as I'm typing this on my computer? It's just now turning 4:13 p.m. on this sunny, hot, humid Friday afternoon in Cincinnati, Ohio. I'm encouraged right now, though the enemy is raging around me, I can do all things through Christ! And so can you!

It is a myth that Satan is the source of all our problems. He is part of the source, but we are the other part. Ever since the fall of man, when Eve convinced Adam to eat what God had told them not to eat, man has turned his heart away from God. And we are still doing that today. Zechariah 7:12 tells us, *"They made their hearts as hard as the hardest stone. They wouldn't listen to the law. They wouldn't pay attention to the Lord's messages."*

We have a choice; our free will. And we tend to pick the wrong choices first. We pick what the world offers before we pick what God offers. And that causes a hardening of the heart. And, as the heart hardens, our ability to choose the right things diminishes. And, from the evil that creeps into our heart, we make those wrong choices.

Even though all that is evil, including manipulation, originally comes from Satan, we allow it to come into our hearts, and that shows we often cause our own hurt. So don't blame it all on Satan, sometimes it's your own fault!

Stop and discern. Can you see when the enemy has released an attack to bring division among The Church? You must stand against this attack. Do not entertain the temptation to be offended, to point the finger in accusation, or respond with manipulation. You must deal with your own heart and be righteous. This is a time to refocus your attention to the Lord. For, He will extricate you from offense if you will allow it. Proverbs 18:19 says, *"A brother offended is harder to win than a strong city, and contentions are like the bars of a castle."*

With all of that being said. . . Satan does carry out his plans of accomplishing evil using mankind. [4] He gets into the hearts and minds of good men and women and uses them as tools of manipulation. So who are these people? Knowing that Satan is the source, who does he use as his puppets? That brings us to the next chapter. . . BUT FIRST. . .

<u>**Time to Get Real. . .**</u>

1. How does it make you feel knowing that Satan is the original source of all evil and manipulation?
2. How does Satan carry out his evil plans?

218

3. Has Satan ever gotten into your head manipulating you to feel a certain way?

4. Have you ever acted in an ungodly way as a result of Satan's manipulation?

5. What encouragement does Philippians 4:13 give us?

6. What part does "free will" play when making choices?

7. What kind of responsibility do you think we, as believers, have when it comes to protecting our minds, motivations, and will?

8. Marc Bell, a great friend of mine says, *"We all have a bucket. We chose what we are going to fill it up with."* What are you filling yours with?

Chapter 11

"Spiritual Manipulators, Stand Up and Admit It"

"Spiritual Manipulators, Stand Up and Admit It"

*A*s you have seen in the last chapter, we only have one enemy - and it's not each other; it's the devil. Satan is the principal source of all evil and manipulation. However, he does carry out his plans through mankind, using us as puppets.

How often in our Church history have we assembled in our respective houses of corporate worship, listening to preachers pleading with us to affirm their message? How many times have you heard the preacher ask you to repeat his/her "Amen?"

How many times have we been spiritually manipulated into giving our finances for our tithes, offerings, or special fund raising campaign? How often have we been manipulated into coming down to an altar to respond to *"the call"* given by the spiritual leader? How often have we been influenced by an emotional reaction to the music to do something or say something we might not necessarily have done otherwise?

Please don't get me wrong. I believe God does, and will continue to use certain individuals in our lives, like preachers, etc. to stir us into making decisions for the benefit of the Kingdom. As well, I know without a doubt God has and will continue to use spiritual leaders like pastors, evangelists, musicians, etc. to draw people to a place of eternal decisions for Christ by the Holy Spirit.

The Spirit of God does move when the Body of Christ comes together to worship Him, and I'm all for it! In fact, bring it on! The problem I have is when someone in their own flesh attempts to spiritually manipulate others for the sake of their own gain in some way, shape, or form.

Also, it gets my goat when this type of manipulation is primarily used to influence people to make what we think is a Kingdom decision, and it's not. Plain and simple, manipulation is wrong and it must stop. Especially within the ranks of the Church! Spiritual manipulators . . . stand up and admit your manipulative ways to God and repent!

Before we can go any further. . .

Before we can go any further, we must quickly deal with an issue that has been bugging me for years. It's the issue concerning the so-called difference between the "clergy" and the "laity." It has always bothered me when people would talk about the distinction between the two, as if the clergy were the ones in a higher position, and the laity was the poor sheep sitting in the pews just waiting to be told what to do. As if it weren't for the clergy, the sheep would be wandering aimlessly through life, with no understanding of their divine destiny in God, right? Wrong!

Some "clergy" members are like Thor making demands of the people as we see in the Movie THOR. . .

Famous Movie Quote:

2011 Movie THOR[1]

[As Thor is stuffing his face with food]

Jane Foster: *"How'd you get inside that cloud?"*

Darcy Lewis: *"Also how could you eat an entire box of Pop Tarts and still be this hungry?"*

[Thor doesn't reply instead finishes chewing and drinking his coffee]

Thor: *"This drink, I like it!"*

Darcy Lewis: *"I know, it's great, right?"*

[Thor suddenly throws his coffee cup to the ground shattering the mug]

Thor: *"Another!"*

In the beginning, when Jesus started what we now know as the Church, there was never a distinction between the laity and the clergy. That was never God's plan to begin with. God did give us the "Five Fold Ministry Gifts" mentioned in Ephesians 4:11, *"And He gave some, apostles; and some, prophets; and some evange-lists; and some, pastors and teachers."* But the fact remains that He created the Body to be equal. Man made the distinction between the two, laity and clergy, thus I believe we've set leaders up to become manipulators without even realizing it.

Some Christians attend gatherings in which a distinction is made between the "clergy" and the "laity", while others attend gatherings at which no such distinction is made. So how and when did this distinction come about? And is it Biblical?

Let us first consider the Greek forms, definitions, and Biblical uses of these words.[2] The Greek form of the word "clergy" is "kleros", which James Strong defines as "heritage, inheritance, lot, part" in his <u>Dictionary of Bible Words</u>. It is used 13 times in the New Testament for the following:

- the "lots" cast for Jesus' vesture (Matthew 27:35, Mark 15:24, Luke 23:24, and John 19:24)
- Judas Iscariot's "part" in service (Acts 1:17); the "part" of the service and apostleship from which Judas fell (Acts 1:25)
- the "lots" given on Barsabas and Matthias, and the "lot" which fell on Matthias (Acts 1:26)
- the "lot" which Simon did not have (Acts 8:21)

- the "inheritance" which saved Gentiles receive (Acts 26:18); the "inheritance" which the saints share (Colossians 1:12)

- members of the flock, God's "heritage" or "allotment", whom the elders are to shepherd and not to lord over (1 Peter 5:3)

The Greek form of the word "laity" is "laos", which Strong's Concordance defines simply as "people". It is used 143 times in the New Testament – in Matthew 2:6 for God's "people" Israel; in Luke 2:31 for all "peoples", before whose face God has prepared His salvation; in Romans 9:24-26 for Gentile "people" whom God has called; in 1 Peter 2:9-10 for a "people" for a possession, God's "people"; in Revelation 14:6 for every "people" to whom the everlasting gospel is preached; and in Revelation 21:3 for God's "people" with whom He will dwell eternally.

So *kleros* and *laos* are clearly Biblical concepts. But there is no suggestion in scripture that the *kleros* are a class or group of persons *distinct* from the *laos*.

Church historian Charles Jacobs writes in <u>The Story of the Church</u>,[3] "In the beginning most of the work of the congregation was done by people who had no official position. It was voluntary service, freely rendered. By the middle of the third century, it was done by the professional clergy. Between clergymen and laity there was a sharp distinction. The clergy, too, were divided into higher and lower grades. In the higher grades were bishops, presbyters and

225

deacons; in the lower grade sub-deacons, lectors, exorcists, acolytes, and janitors. All of them were inducted into office by some form of ordination, and the idea of local organization had gone so far that in some churches even the gravediggers were ordained. Thus the work of the Church was passing out of the hands of the many into those of the few, and these few were coming to be regarded as belonging to a higher class."

Let me encourage you to take note of the following portions of scripture. (NKJV)

Matthew 18:20 *For where two or three are gathered together in My name, there am I there in the midst of them.*

Matthew 23:8-10 *But you, do not be called 'Rabbi'; for One is your Teacher, the Christ, and you are all brethren. Do not call anyone on earth your father; for One is your Father, He who is in heaven. And do not be called teachers; for One is your Teacher, the Christ.*

Romans 12:4-8 *For as we have many members in one body, but all the members do not have the same function, so we, being many, are one body in Christ, and individually members of one another. Having then gifts differing according to the grace that is given to us, let us use them: if prophecy, let us prophesy in proportion to our faith; or ministry, let us use it in our ministering; he who teaches, in teaching; he who exhorts, in exhortation; he who gives, with liberality; he who leads, with diligence; he who shows mercy, with cheerfulness.*

1 Corinthians 14:26-33 *How is it then, brethren? Whenever you come together, each of you has a psalm, has a teaching, has a tongue, has a revelation, has an interpretation. Let all things be done for edification. If anyone speaks in a tongue, let there be two or at the most three, each in turn, and let one interpret. But if there is no interpreter, let him keep silent in church, and let him speak to himself and to God. Let two or three prophets speak, and let the others judge. But if anything is revealed to another who sits by, let the first keep silent. For you can all prophesy one by one, that all may learn and all may be encouraged. And the spirits of the prophets are subject to the prophets. For God is not the author of confusion but of peace, as in all the churches of the saints.*

Hebrews 8:1-2 *Now this is the main point of the things we are saying: We have such a High Priest, who is seated at the right hand of the throne of the Majesty in the heavens, a Minister of the sanctuary and of the true tabernacle which the Lord erected, and not man.*

1 Peter 2:4-5 *Coming to Him as to a living stone, rejected indeed by men, but chosen by God and precious, you also, as living stones, are being built up a spiritual house, a holy priesthood, to offer up spiritual sacrifices acceptable to God through Jesus Christ.*

Revelation 1:5-6 *From Jesus Christ, the faithful witness, the firstborn from the dead, and the ruler over the kings of the earth. To Him who loved us and washed us from our sins in His own blood, and has made us kings and priests to His God and Father, to Him be glory and dominion forever and ever. Amen.*

It is my prayer that we can simply be The Church. That we can come together as a family on a regular basis to celebrate who Jesus Christ is in our lives and enjoy His presence in our midst. All true Christians are God's people (laos), His inheritance (kleros). And Jesus is Minister of the sanctuary, our great High Priest, our glorious living Head, our Instructor, and our Savior.

Currently, it is what it is

With that being said, let's face it, the Church is where it is and more than likely will continue to maintain the separation between the clergy and the laity. Leaders, let's move toward the direction God would have us as declared in scripture, and not what we want to set up as structure because of any manipulative, power hungry attitudes. In the meantime, what can we do about it until that changes?

Within the structure of the modern day Church and while each of us, no matter our position in The Church, has the ability to manipulate others, I've chosen to focus on spiritual leaders. They have the potential to impact more people *because* of their position. If you see some of these attitudes in your own life, please be quick to repent and move forward in freedom.

228

As we look at the people who are actually being used by the enemy to spiritually manipulate others (whether they realize it or not), you might have a tendency to think I came up with this list from the example of people in our own Church, or ones we have been a part of in the past. Well, rest assured, I did not.

I'm not saying we haven't dealt with our share of abuses over the past, for I am the guiltiest of them all. But I am pleased to say (for the most part) that the people within our own Church family set a wonderful example in how to treat others with respect, truth, and love, not with manipulation.

Who are those most likely to be used by the enemy for his purpose of control, manipulation and abuse; remembering we have only one enemy. It is the devil . . . not each other? Here we go. (In no particular order.)

#1: Pastors

Case in point. The youth pastor of the local Church in town is planning to take their students on a missions trip oversees. A lot of money will have to be raised in order for the students to be able to go. Of course, the senior pastor told the youth pastor to put enough money in the budget to pay for his expenses too. So youth pastor Larry wants to raise as much as possible in order to make sure he can have an expense-free trip as well as help out his own personal budget at the same time.

Youth pastor Larry finds as many heartfelt, tear-jerking pictures of impoverished children in the area to which they are going. He enters them onto his *iMac* and makes the most beautiful, emotionally-charged movie he can possibly make, hoping to trigger his desired response. He shows it to the congregation one Sunday. They take up an offering and voilà! The money comes in.

Youth Pastor Larry is praising God in public for the finances coming in, but down deep, he knows that he just manipulated the Church into giving. But of course he justifies it in his mind because after all, *it's for the Kingdom*, right?

It's plain and simple, manipulation.

How about the senior pastor of the local Church who would love to have his house painted and doesn't want to spend his own time, energy, and money to make it happen? So what do you hear when sitting in your usual seat week after week in your place of worship? You hear small hints that the pastor's favorite color is orange and he'd love to have an orange house. Or, wouldn't it be wonderful if the Church body could come together on a project? And then laughingly adds, "You know my house could sure use a fixing up. You know how much I want to set a good example in the community for excellence! Ha, ha, ha."

And wouldn't you know it, after a few weeks, the men's ministry puts together a workday. Low and behold, where do they want to start? The pastor's house!

Check it off the list pastor, now you can move to more spiritual undertakings and not have to worry about such earthly things as painting your house. Hey, the Church body is there to do things like that for you! It's a love gift after all!

Arrrggghhhhh!

Don't forget, I'm a pastor! I've been there. <u>I've done it</u>. It happens.

Again, hear my heart Church. If you want to paint your pastor's house, mow his yard or even buy him a new motorcycle; then go for it! Bless him or her and their family. Give honor and blessings to whom honor is do. But for Pete's sake, don't do it because you've been manipulated into doing it. Do it because you love them and want to bless them. Do it because you consider them to be a friend and you'd be more than happy to do whatever you can for any friend in need.

Forgive me for this one.

Forgive me, but I must share this personal example. I know a pastor who purchased a number of "fixer upper" houses and then manipulated certain members of the congregation who had house-building skills to help him fix them up. Basically, they did all of the work, and of course, for free. The pastor then turned around and sold those houses, pocketed the money and didn't even think about blessing those who did the work for him! But the sad thing is, they

231

did that work for him because they loved him and wanted to serve him in whatever capacity they could. Their hearts were right; the pastor's was not.

Pastors, we need to knock it off. It's manipulation.

#2: Vision Casters

The Bible clearly states in Proverbs 29:18 (AMP) *Where there is no vision, nor redemptive revelation of God, the people perish.* We are instructed as well to write it down and make it clear so it can be heralded to all. Vision casting needs to be done. Our spiritual leaders need to catch a vision from God and share it with us. We need the genuine "Moses figures" in our lives to share with us the direction the Lord is leading. Vision is necessary for all of us to have if we are going to make an impact for God to corporately change the culture in which we live.

The problem I have with some "vision casting" however, is when it is presented in a manipulative way to get people to give of their hard earned time, talent, and treasure towards something that will make the visionary look good and not for the Glory of God. Sure, it's all wrapped up in Godly verbiage and churchy metaphors that make sense. And sure, the vision is something that would be wonderful to see come to pass, if it really happens. But is the vision really something from God or just a manipulative person or group of people that call themselves leaders in our Churches attempting to make a name for themselves or push their own personal agendas through with the purpose of gaining popularity, control, or personal wealth?

As my friend Todd says, "I'm just sayin'."

Yes, yes, yes! Let's cast vision, fellow vision casters. But may we do it in a way that is truthful, pure, Biblical, and non-manipulative. If it's really a God given vision, we shouldn't have to manipulate it in a way to "sell" it. Either the Church will buy into it because it's a God thing or they won't. I believe our responsibility is to be true to God, true to the vision, true to ourselves, and the Church.

Church body, you do need to do your part when a vision for your future has been presented to you. You need to spend the right amount of time in the presence of God to know whether or not this is a vision you can give your life to or not. If it is, then go for it. If not, then don't. But decide for yourself and not because of others. Don't allow yourself to be manipulated or pressured into giving of your time, talents, and treasure towards the vision if you're not for it. You'll be spending your time and resources on a dead horse and will eventually become disgruntled when the horse doesn't start running.

Vision Casters, we need to knock it off. It's manipulation.

#3: Preachers

I stand guilty of this. I am a preacher of the Gospel and I am guilty of spiritually abusing the Church. As I stated before, I have and still do repent for it. It's a bad habit that is easy to get into, especially after watching and listening to so many of my predecessors do the same thing over the years. It seems we preachers have our own language that is just "weird" some times.

And you know what? I've noticed when preaching to a group of people that it's a whole lot more fun when the listeners are actively involved with what I'm saying. When I get their feedback, it makes me feel good about what I'm saying and it makes me feel great that they are more than likely enjoying themselves and agreeing with me.

When the listeners are quiet, I get the feeling they are bored with me, not listening, and really don't look at me as being a "Man of God bringing forth Truth for such a time as this."

So what do I do to make me feel better about myself and my method of delivery? I try to evoke responses from them. I do this by saying in a one-word question at the end of my powerful point, "Amen?". If they don't say it loud enough then I ask it again, "Amen?!".

Maybe you'll recall some of these colloquialisms or idioms you may have heard as preachers have waxed on so eloquently. . .

"Now don't get quiet on me just because I'm preaching good now."
"Can I get a witness tonight?"
"Can I hear an amen?"
"This is good preaching even if I'm preaching to myself."
"Say amen or oh me; you've got to say something."
"Are you picking up what I'm laying down?"
"Am I preaching to the choir this morning?"

Listen, I get it. Sometimes we preachers, because of our own insecurities, need to be assured by others we're doing well. We all need affirmation, and the Bible even tells us to affirm one another. I get it. I know what the Word of the Lord says. . .

Proverbs 12:18 (AMP) *There are those who speak rashly, like the piercing of a sword, but the tongue of the wise brings healing.*

Proverbs 16:24 (AMP) *Pleasant words are as a honeycomb, sweet to the mind and healing to the body.*

Ephesians 4:29 (NKJV) *Let no corrupt word proceed out of your mouth, but what is good for necessary edification, that it may impart grace to the hearers.*

Don't get me wrong, affirmation is a good thing to give when you're listening to a preacher share the Word. Galatians 6:6 (NKJV). *Let him who is taught the word share in all good things with him who teaches.* I will be the first to give my pastor an "Amen" when he says something that I agree with! Feel free to be an encourager, a spark plug, and a fire starter within your congregation. Tell your pastor or leader they did well; affirm them; it's your responsibility. But be careful when affirmation is being elicited for the sole purpose of manipulating you into buying into their message for the sake of their own personal pleasure, gratification, or ego. We have to draw the line somewhere, don't we?

Can I get an Amen?

Sadly, when we pass our spiritual authority onto the next, as in the account of Elijah and Elisha, we also pass on some of our bad habits and characteristics that are not scriptural. And I'm sad to say our manipulative preaching jargon goes on that list.

Preachers, we need to knock it off. It's manipulation.

#4: Evangelists

Can I say this at least one more time, Arrrggghhhhh!

Hey, I love the gift of the evangelist and have even walked in that gifting many times. The evangelist is needed in the Church body and I pray more are raised up as the Church moves forward to change the culture. The office of the evangelist is a part of the five-fold ministry we must embrace within our local Church bodies. It's a God thing.

The problem I've had in the past is when the evangelist comes in, stirs up the pot, messes with emotions, takes up a second offering, tells us he loves us, and then leaves town! Isn't it amazing how the office of the evangelist has taken on such a bad reputation in the past, and now you hardly see any of the younger generation of Christ followers walking in that anointing or desire to.

Never again pal. Don't even think about it!

I remember an evangelist coming to our Church on one occasion, and we invited everyone in town to come and hear him. He was supposed to be the next best-anointed man of God who would change everything. He was on worldwide television and seemed to have a pretty cool handle on how to "*do*" ministry. He was looked upon by many in the Church world as a B-MOG: a "Big Man of God." If a pastor could just get him to come to their church, then they'd see real revival take place!

We invited one particular group in the community my bride had made a connection with to come to the service. They called themselves "*The Alternatives*." My bride, Butch, had a true connection with these youth type young people with blue, red and green spiked hair. They would come to her meetings with the smell of pot and other substances upon them, and ready to listen to what she had to say. Together they built a bridge of mutual respect and love for each other. She loved and respected them and they loved and respected her.

My bride was able to minister God's love to them; it was real and genuine, and best of all, received. They received her love and were in the process of becoming more like Christ every day. She had a level of trust built with them that was pure and growing.

She decided to invite her group to hear this evangelist. They came the first night simply because they loved, respected, and trusted Butch. They, as well as we, thought this was going to be a life-changing event for *"The Alternatives."*

It was life changing all right, but not the right kind of change. The evangelist, when given the microphone, started his message by talking about money. He not only talked about it, he did everything he could to manipulate the Church into giving to his ministry. He spent the first full hour talking about money. Then he said a few novice things about something else, took up his offering, and it was over. The whole night was about money and that was it!

Butch and I were devastated. From that very moment, the bridge she had painstakingly made with the students was torn apart. It took months to repair the damage that had been done. *The Alternatives* wanted nothing to do with a Church like that (all about money.)

The manipulation of the evangelist that night did more harm to those students who were genuinely seeking for answers in their lives through a relationship with God than any one person should be able to do. It was wrong. It was ungodly. Needless to say, that was the evangelist's only night there and he's never been invited back. Never again pal. Don't even think about it!

Here's the deal as a pastor. I love our Church body and value them as if they were my own children. I want nothing but God's absolute best for their lives in every way possible. I want to see them walk and love in the fullness of God's blessings, as they fulfill their Kingdom Assignments. I want to see their relationships blessed, their marriages secure, their finances beyond the top, their dreams and desires all met. I want to see them walk in authority and confidence in the power of the Holy Spirit, every day and night of their lives. I want to see them move beyond the expectations of man and those who seek their demise. I want to see them make a **True Impact** for the Kingdom of God. I DESIRE TO DO WHATEVER I POSSIBLY CAN TO HELP MAKE THAT HAPPEN!

Even as Thor desired something to ride as seen in this movie quote; so is my desire to see the Body of Christ rise above manipulation.

Famous Movie Quote:

2011 Movie THOR[4]

[walking into a pet shop]

Thor: *"I need a horse!"*
Pet Store Clerk: *"We don't have horses. Just dogs, cats, birds."*
Thor: *"Then give me one of those large enough to ride!"*

Church, stand up and don't allow yourself to be messed with by someone who is trying to manipulate you!

Evangelists, we need to knock it off. It's manipulation.

#5: Televangelists

It is not my intention to name names in a public forum as this. If I did, then I would be adding to the divisional ways of the enemy. But I would like to name one name that I believe all of us can learn from. His example in how to <u>not</u> be a manipulator is outstanding. It's Billy Graham. Perhaps, for some of you reading this, you may have personal issues with Mr. Graham, which I respect. But for me, I consider him to be one of my spiritual heroes of the faith. I wish I could say that about other televangelists, but the fact is, there are some out there who are manipulating their way into the hearts and minds of the Church for the purpose of their own personal gain.

Remember, I believe there are some televangelists who are outstanding men and women of God and making a wonderful, beautiful, pure impact in the world today; but there are some who are not; and we must be aware of them.

While in Africa on one of our mission trips, Rev. Graham had just left the area where we were ministering. One of the local pastors was in his meetings and he told me how impressed he was that Rev. Graham spoke a simple message each night and that he wore the same suit every night as well! He was amazed how a man of his stature was not caught up in the glam and glitz of clothes and jewelry, and just lived a plain simple life. He loved the fact that he only had one suit. Now I'm sure Rev. Graham had more than one suit, but the impression my pastor friend had was that it was his only suit. He saw this as a form of humility and grace. By not wearing a different flashy designer suit with all the gold and frills every night (which is often the culture of some evangelists), he set an example for us all.

I have always kept dear to my heart the response Rev. Graham gave to a reporter who asked him the reason for his success in the ministry. How did he stay out of the eye of controversy and scandal? His response, "I don't touch the women, the money, or the glory." [5] He is an example of humility to me in my ministry.

Use your own discernment, Church, when watching those on television who are sharing God's Word with you. When you're asked for money or given a plea to help with a project, use wisdom. Don't just buy into it because you "*feel*" like it's the right thing to do. There are some good ones out there, but some of these folks will manipulate you right into giving them your life savings if you allow them.

Televangelists, we need to knock it off. It's manipulation.

#6: Elders/Deacons/Trustees/Board

Give them whatever title you want, you know who I'm talking about. If you have been a part of Church life for any time at all, you've probably experienced the manipulation from some of this group of leaders. It's sad but true, that there has been more than one set of these folks who has manipulated Church members into taking a side contrary to another, causing a split in the Church family. My heart will forever hurt for those innocent Church members that have had nothing to do with Church politics and been ripped away from Church family members that they love. It's not right. It's not fair, and it's ungodly in every aspect.

I have a pastor friend who shared with me how he was having problems with the Church board. They wanted to control everything.

241

The board wanted to tell him what to do, when to do it, and how it should be done. They went behind his back and manipulated other Church members into believing that, even though he was a *great guy* and they *loved him dearly*, he was living a life of sin; which he was not (and later proved to be the case). Of course it broke their hearts to have to share this news. But they had to speak the truth. It was their *"spiritual duty"* as a board member.

To top it off, when my pastor friend got up to speak on a Sunday morning, one of these board members would actually turn their chair around in the sanctuary and face the opposite direction of the pastor. It was unbelievable the type of control and manipulation they were attempting to practice.

And as the story would go, the Church body split with some members taking the side of the pastor and others the side of the board. I'm sure that's not the way God intended for the Church to operate. We are a family. We all have different forms of government within our Church and that's fine. The problem occurs when one or more of the members of the Church government begin to manipulate others into doing something, saying something, or being something that is contrary to God's plan for the Church body. When one or more of the members of any Church government begin to pursue their own personal gain or to push their particular agenda through, it's manipulation.

Elders/Deacons/Trustees/Board or whatever your title, we need to knock it off. It's manipulation.

#7: Leaders Holding Secrets

Another disturbing common denominator in identifying spiritual abuse, and manipulation of the Church is found in leaders who have a paranoid desire for secrecy. They often hide executive decisions and operations behind a strict "need-to-know" policy.

This reminds me of the Spiderman movie when Aunt May is speaking to his nephew Ben Parker. . .

Famous Movie Quote:

2012 Movie THE AMAZING SPIDERMAN [6]
(talking to Peter Parker after he won't share the truth why he was acting strange)
Aunt May: *"Secrets have a cost; they're not for free. Not now. Not ever."*

Financial records and administrative decisions are often hidden from the prying eyes and questioning minds of "lesser" church members or outsiders. When, however, that proves impossible, the more ambiguous or questionable items in the church budget, such as salaries and ministerial expenses, are covertly grouped or obscured to hide factual information from general scrutiny. Clear future plans are seldom revealed to the congregation except in their most palatable and agreeable parts. Loyalty to the leaders and conformity to the rules of the organization are repeatedly stressed and all decisions regarding expenditures and policy are left to the wisdom and discretion of the "anointed" few. Clear lines of authority, complete with flow charts, are drawn and reinforced, usually by the person at the top of the list. Now if this doesn't drive you crazy, nothing will.

Leaders Holding Secrets, we need to knock it off. It's manipulation.

#8: Worship Leaders and Musicians

I have found from personal experience the power that music has over people. Music is purposely used to manipulate our emotions on a daily basis, including within the walls of our Church celebrations. I'm a musician. I've used music to sway others. I've played my sax to my wife hoping to bring her around to meeting my desires. I can play a mean sexy sax and manipulate the ears of those listening if I wanted to. I know firsthand the power that music has over a person.

Have you ever noticed that doctor's office waiting rooms play music to calm you down? Bars and nightclubs play music to rile you up? Have you ever watched a movie with no music behind it? Probably not. It's the music that endears our hearts to the emotion the directors are trying to stir up.

Take the movie, "*Castaway*" starring Tom Hanks . . . If you've seen the movie, you'll notice the high energy, powerful, emotional music that flows at the beginning and ending of the movie. But as soon as Chuck Nolan sets foot on the island, the music stops. The entire time he is on the island as a castaway there is not one sound made outside of the natural sounds of the island itself and Nolan's voice. Not even Wilson speaks a single word!

Music impacts to say the least. I can remember when I proposed to my bride, asking for her hand in marriage. We were on the shores of beautiful Lake Washington in Seattle. I had previously and secretly arranged for my roommates to set up a make shift tent that I would eventually persuade my future, incredibly reluctant wife to enter. When we walked up to the tent, my roommates pushed the "Play" button on the special tape I had made especially for that night. It was a tape of romantic love songs like, *Isn't She Lovely* and *Once, Twice, Three times a Lady*.

How could she resist my romanticism and my thoughtful heart to provide not only this wonderful music for the night, but a bucket of *Kentucky Fried Chicken* to go with it?!

As the music played, I held her in my arms, a soft breeze blowing across the lake, a lantern glowing upon her lovely face, a light mist in the air and Lionel Ritchie! I had her at "Will".

And she answered with, "Yes Please!"

Music is powerfully persuasive. In the Bible, David played the harp to sooth the soul of the King. 1 Samuel 16:23 (NIV) *Whenever the spirit from God came upon Saul, David would take his harp and play. Then relief would come to Saul; he would feel better, and the evil spirit would leave him.*

245

Music can set an atmosphere and create an environment for almost anything. Why do you think we preachers ask the musicians to come forward at the end of our messages? We are not just trying to give the listeners hope that we have almost finished our message and that the signal for musicians is their sign of assurance. The reason is because we know the impact the music will have on your hearts as you listen to what we are saying.

Now I'm not saying that's all bad, for the Holy Spirit speaks to our hearts through the medium of music. Music at the end of a message can be and should be used as a way to create an environment that will be conducive for the Holy Spirit to speak to the hearts of the Church and those in attendance who do not have a relationship with Jesus Christ. After all, God created all music; did He not? But when it's used to manipulate for the purpose of satisfying human ego, it's wrong and spiritually abusive. God created it in its most pure form. The motives of men have twisted and shaped it into a tool and device for manipulation and control.

Musicians, never use your gift to manipulate the Church for your own means, but use your gift to edify the Father and create an environment in which the Holy Spirit can move.

Preachers, never use music as a way to rouse the emotions of the Church so that you can look good, sound good, or get people emotionally charged to "Amen" you. Use the music as you preach to create an environment where the Holy Spirit can speak to challenge, edify, and encourage the Church.

The African Elephant Dance

I would have to say the purist form of Holy Spirit orchestrated music I've ever heard coming forth through the Church was during one of our services in the Philippines in April of 2012. One evening I shared with the Church, about 3,000 members strong, a teaching on the African elephant dance and the correlation of their dance in how it would relate to us, the Church.

It's an amazing thing, how these elephants that God created find water in the African desert. A herd of elephants in the desert, thirsty and searching for water, will separate to look for it. They will search until they find water or sense an underground spring. They can sense water up to 8 feet below the surface of the ground. It is a natural sense of survival instinct created by God. The desire to live is incredible; and without water, they will die.

When one elephant senses water under the ground, that elephant sends out a sound that is eight octaves lower than the human ear can detect. That sound, that crying out, carries up to 40 miles in distance. Suddenly, all the other elephants within the 40-mile radius can hear the cry and come to the one who is crying out. When all of the elephants come together, they begin to dance upon the dry, hard ground. As they dance in unity together, the ground begins to break and the waters begin to gush out. The elephants then drink to their hearts' content.

The night I shared this in the Philippines, there was no man-made music being played. I shared the true story of the African Elephant

Dance and then just waited. After about 10 minutes of silence a cry began to come from the hearts of the people. It started with one soul as he cried out to the Lord. The sound began to spread upon others until everyone was crying out to God. There was a *"deep crying unto deep"* experience that came out of the hearts and mouths of the people. This was a sound I will never forget as they pressed into the manifest presence of God Almighty, awaiting His direction and pace!

The sound built and became stronger and then would lessen in its volume even as the waves of the ocean would come and go. It would build into a tense and obvious fervor of the Spirit only to become quiet and calming moments later. The sound of the move of the Spirit was in the house – and no one was playing any instruments! God orchestrated all of it! In fact, if someone would have been playing, it probably wouldn't have happened.

Music can manipulate. Musicians can manipulate. Yes, let's build an atmosphere conducive for the Spirit of God to move, but if we're trying to manipulate people into doing something for any other reason outside of bringing God glory – it's wrong.

Worship Leaders and Musicians, we need to knock it off. It's manipulation.

#9: Those who Misuse Scripture

Have you ever listened to someone preach a message and just assumed what they were saying certainly had to be backed up by the Bible? More often than not, because of our love and acceptance for the person who is sharing the message, we give them the benefit of the doubt what they share is Biblically sound. We have a tendency to say to ourselves, "That sounds right" and don't even check to see if it is or not.

At Eastgate, we put an outline of the sermon in our weekly bulletins so the Church family can take notes. I always add scripture to my points to support what I'm going to say. One time a Church family member came up to me prior to the service and said, "Pastor, I just wanted to show you that one of your scriptures today is wrong." He was very respectful, polite, and quite humble when he told me, for which I thanked him and thought, "Wow, some people really do check out if what I say is right or not!" I checked it out, and he was right! From that time on, I've always double and sometimes triple checked my notes to make sure I'm not preaching something not properly supported by the Word.

What I find to be just as serious however is the flagrant (if not fraudulent) frequent misuse of scripture employed by authoritarian religious leaders to support their claim to pre-eminence and privilege. This, despite the New Testament's clear instruction that those who lead are first and foremost servants. 2 Corinthians 4:5 (NLT) *We don't go around preaching about ourselves; we preach Christ Jesus, the Lord. All we say about ourselves is that we are your servants because of what Jesus has done for us.* When selfless service is usurped by a compelling ambition for narcissistic control, abusive leadership naturally results. Misusing scripture for one's own selfish ends invariably

249

cultivates a malignant climate of legalistic control. Sadly it fosters unnecessary (and sometimes destructive) guilt among members who fail to attribute proper "honor" to their leader. They "twist" (2 Pet.3.16) the scriptures to fit their own preconceptions (misconceptions) of leadership or, like Diotrephes of old (3 John 1:9), their lust for "preeminence" has earned them the censure of scripture.

2 Peter 3:16 (NLT) *Speaking of these things in all of his letters. Some of his comments are hard to understand, and those who are ignorant and unstable have twisted his letters around to mean something quite different from what he meant, just as they do the other parts of Scripture — and the result is disaster for them.*

3 John 1:9 (NLT) *I sent a brief letter to the church about this, but Diotrephes, who loves to be the leader, does not acknowledge our authority.*

I like what Brennan Manning says as he delivers a staggering knockout blow to the 21st Century Church when he writes, "No greater sinners exist than those so-called Christians who disfigure the face of God, mutilate the gospel of grace, and intimidate others through fear. They corrupt the essential nature of Christianity." [7] Ouch!

Those Who Misuse Scripture, we need to knock it off. It's manipulation.

#10: Self-Proclaimed Titled Leaders

Wow. You want to know what really bugs me? (Or should I say Arrrggghhhhh!) It's those individuals, acting in the name of God, who have given themselves "self proclaimed titles." I can't stand it. They give themselves a title they believe will bring them honor. They believe that if they have the title, then the respect of the people will come with it. It's manipulation and it's wrong. Church, watch out for such deception. The title is given in such secrecy that hardly anyone is even aware of it! We blindly accept their title as if it were legitimate (and most of the time it is), but sometimes, it's not.

For example, I know one such person that was able to convince a small group of people into calling him an Apostle. So what did he do? He put it on his business card. "Apostle such and such." Another was able to get an organization to give him/her an honorary degree to make the person seem more educated or more "honorable".

If you need to have a title to prove you have authority, you really don't have authority. If you feel like the Church body won't respect you unless you have a title, you really don't deserve their respect. Titles don't bring authority; but what you do, for whom you do it, and the motive behind why you do it brings authority. Your badge doesn't give you authority; the person who gives you the badge gives you authority. The badge then just represents the authority already been given you.

I love this quote from the movie SPIDERMAN as Peter parker in a voiceover is speaking. . .

Famous Movie Quote:

2002 Movie SPIDERMAN [8]

Peter Parker: *"Whatever life holds in store for me, I will never forget these words: 'With great power comes great responsibility.' This is my gift, my curse. Who am I? I'm Spider-man."*

This could be reworded for the Church, "Whatever life holds in store for me, I will never forget these words: 'With great power comes great responsibility.' This is my gift from God. Who am I? I'm a member of The Church!"

Church, the badge doesn't bring power. God is the one who gives power and strength to His servants and the authority of His presence follows. But with that authority and power comes great responsibility for all of us.

Self-proclaimed titles of authority are manipulative and will not hold up when in a battle. Either you are what you are because God has made you what you are, or you are not. When the devil comes against you with all of the force of hell, your self-proclaimed authority will quickly become useless. The devil knows who has Godly authority and who does not.

Acts 19:15 (ESV) *But the evil spirit answered them, "Jesus I know, and Paul I recognize, but who are you?"*

To be honest with you, there was a time in my ministry when I really wanted people to call me "Pastor." If they didn't use the title "Pastor" before my name, I thought they were being disrespectful. It used to bug me, but I'm over it. The reason is, if that person feels in their heart that I am their Pastor, they'll call me Pastor if they want to. And if they don't, that's okay, because I still know that I am a

Pastor. I don't have to hear them say it in order to believe it. I know my calling and I know my giftings, regardless whether I'm called by that title or not.

I understand some people do feel disrespectful if they don't use titles when referring to or talking to someone. I honor that. If that's your heart to call someone by his or her title, then do it. For example, I would never call my pastor by his first name alone. Why? Because for me and the culture in which I grew up, that wasn't done. I would feel uncomfortable not including his title. But if you do, it's okay. Just be careful that you're not calling them that title simply because they manipulated the means by which they got it.

You can call me Dave if you want to

In my travels overseas I noticed when one of the local pastors I've known for years called me "papa." He considered me to be his spiritual father and called me that as a sign of respect, "Papa Dave." All my life I've been called either Dave or Dale, both of which are who I am. Suddenly, to my surprise everyone in that area began calling me "Papa." And through the course of time, the title has more recently changed to "Apostle." I never asked to be called one. I never called myself one. Nor will I. But many began calling me their Apostle. Now, after many years in the field, planting my life into leaders and pastors of Churches overseas, I am most often referred to as their "Apostle."

I am honored and humbled to be given a title by such loving people. Do I feel worthy? No. Do I feel I deserve it? No. Do I strive to hear it? No. Will I put it on a business card? No. Will I start a ministry with that in the title? No. Will I create a web site with the title? No. Will I expect people to call me by that title? No. But, am I willing to receive the title as it has been given to me by God and continue to do what I do simply because I love it? Absolutely! If it's a *God* thing – then let it be so! If it's *my* thing – then forget about it!

One more thing; these self-titled, often times abusive leaders, generally stay away from associating with people who are not at least on his/her level because of their "status".

Manipulative, abusive leaders do not feel the need to humble themselves by associating with people of low status. These abusive leaders enjoy setting up barriers to people. By erecting walls around themselves, abusive leaders become more fixated on maintaining their own power than accomplishing God's will for their Church or organization. These leaders tend to only associate with people who can help them advance and prosper. By concentrating on their own interests, abusive, manipulative leaders are loath to spend much time with the needy because they feel those hurting are only impediments to their quest for more power, glory, and prestige.

Many are more concerned about things on earth rather than Christ and His Kingdom. By worrying more about money, materials and possessions, abusive leaders acquire many so-called "idols".

Self-Proclaimed, Titled Leaders, we need to knock it off. It's manipulation.

#11: Those Who Take up the Tithes and Offering

Do I believing in the giving of our tithes and offerings? Without a doubt. Is it part of who we are as believers in Christ? Absolutely. Do I practice tithing and giving of my offerings? Yes. Is it important for us as followers of Christ to give of our finances without restraint to help further the Kingdom of God? No duh!

The problem I have here is one that occurs in almost every worship service on the planet; it is in the way in which it's often times done. Without fail, someone has been assigned to the daunting task of receiving the offering; and it's a tough job! I've been there, done that, got the t-shirt to prove it! It's a tough thing to do. When you have to stand before the people and say just the right thing in order for them to give - that's a lot of pressure!

And the most difficult of tasks is that the person has to receive the offering in a situation where the local Church is hurting financially, or the crusade or meeting that is scheduled is in great need of the money or it will go broke. If the offering isn't enough to cover the expenses, then heads will roll. If the finances don't begin to increase, then we might have to lay off some of our staff. Tough stuff.

Let me remind you of why we give of our monies to the Lord in the first place. We are to give as an act of love to God! My love for God

255

should be so strong and passionate that I can't help but walk in obedience to His Word and direction in my life, which includes my finances. I'm not supposed to give reluctantly or out of persuasion, but out of a passion for God's Presence in my life. I give because I love Him!

When someone stands before you and attempts to manipulate you into giving for any other reason outside of a passion and love for God, watch out. If you feel like you are being persuaded to give outside of the purity of God's Word, then watch out. Don't allow yourself to be taken in by the smooth words of the one asking for the money, no matter how smooth their words may be.

Keep in mind, I've known many fellow ministers who have been assigned to receive the tithes and offerings that particular day and have done it wonderfully well! They mean well and do it with passion and grace. It's done in humility and love. But the moment you feel like you're being manipulated to give, think twice.

Those who take up the weekly tithes and offering, we need to knock it off. It's manipulation.

#12: Those Who Present Potentially Manipulative Formulas

How about those spiritual formulas that people in spiritual authority continue to throw at us. These so-called formulas sound Biblical, but are not. Sure, you can sense the truth behind the saying, but they continue to manipulate us with these formulas as if they were the absolute truths to live by. If we would just do such and such, then such and such would happen automatically in our lives. As if God were some kind of a Genie in a bottle we could rub and He'd automatically have to do whatever it is we ask of Him.

He's not, and He doesn't. Consider this potentially manipulative formula, *"If you have a need, plant a seed."* Is it true? For the most part, sure. Is that a quote from the Bible? No. The Bible does tell us in Luke 6:38 (NKJV), *"Give, and it will be given to you: good measure, pressed down, shaken together, and running over will be put into your bosom. For with the same measure that you use, it will be measured back to you."*

I've come to believe that this verse has been taken out of context quite frequently. If you look at the context, Luke 6:31-42, it is about doing unto others as you would have them do unto you. So if you give good things, and love your enemies, that is what will come back to you with *"good measure, pressed down, shaken together, and running over."* However, if you give judgment, then this also is given back to you with *"good measure, pressed down, shaken together, and running over"* which is a picture the Jews would readily identify with because of the way they bought grain (in some situations the grain was measured out in their laps). Wow! We are really going to get it if we have a life of condemnation and fault finding of others. But also, blessings will come if we are living the life God's called us, to express the Fruit of the Spirit. God tells us He will bring it back on us *"in good measure. . ."*

Take a look at Matthew 7:1-2 (AMP). *"Do not judge and criticize and condemn others, so that you may not be judged and criticized and condemned yourselves. For just as you judge and criticize and condemn others, you will be judged and criticized and condemned, and in accordance with the measure you use to deal out to others, it will be dealt out again to you."*

I have heard Luke 6:38 prayed over people and have even prayed it over people myself before I realized the condemnation I was really asking God to put on them. That's one prayer I hope He didn't answer. Talk about misguided manipulation. . .

The problem is when we preachers say these things as a way of making it seem easy, or if you follow the formula it will automatically happen, or if I can talk you into believing it (manipulation); then I'll look good. Sadly, many preachers take scriptures totally out of context for the sole purpose of enriching themselves - and it sounds cool.

Let me give you a few examples of the potentially manipulative formulas. . .

"Ask anything you want in God's name and He has to do it."
"Name it and claim it."
"Blab it and grab it."
"Once you take care of the sin in your life you will be healed."
"Read one proverb a day and your problems will go away."
"If you'll buy this oil for $20.00 and anoint your house with it, you'll be blessed beyond measure."

Church, when you hear one of these or any other potentially manipulative formulas strike your ears, take to heart the reality and Biblical principles behind it, knowing God is sovereign and will do whatever He desires for our good, whether the formula sounds good or not. If you like and agree with what's being said, then go for it. If you sense you're being manipulated into it for the sake of a feeling, affirmative response to the speaker, or you just want the easy way out; then step back a bit, ask God for wisdom and what your next step should be.

Those who present potentially manipulative formulas, we need to knock it off. It's manipulation.

In a Nutshell

I recently read the Internet blog of *"What If I Stumble"*[9] the following profile contrasting true and false leadership; it may help you to better recognize spiritual abuse: (All verses are found in the NKJV.)

- Abusers drive; leaders lead.

  John 10:11-15 Jesus says, "I am the good shepherd. The good shepherd gives His life for the sheep. But a hireling, he who is not the shepherd, one who does not own the sheep, sees the wolf coming and leaves the sheep and flees; and the wolf catches the sheep and scatters them. The hireling flees because he is a hireling and does not care about the sheep. I am the good shepherd; and I know My sheep, and am known by My own. As the Father knows Me, even so I know the Father; and I lay down My life for the sheep."

- Abusers say, "I"; true leaders say, "We".
  1 Cor. 3:5-9 *Who then is Paul, and who is Apollos, but ministers through whom you believed, as the Lord gave to each one? I planted, Apollos watered, but God gave the increase. So then neither he who plants is anything, nor he who waters, but God who gives the increase. Now he who plants and he who waters are one, and each one will receive his own reward according to his own labor. For we are God's fellow workers; you are God's field, you are God's building.*

- Abusers insist on being served; true leaders serve.
  Matt.23:11 *But he who is greatest among you shall be your servant.*

- Abusers govern by guilt and fear; true leaders create trust.
  1 Thess. 2:10-11 *You are witnesses, and God also, how devoutly and justly and blamelessly we behaved ourselves among you who believe; as you know how we exhorted, and comforted, and charged every one of you, as a father does his own children.*

- Abusers control by guilt and manipulation; true leaders influence by example.

  Phil. 3.17 *Brethren, join in following my example, and note those who so walk, as you have us for a pattern.*

- Abusers think themselves better than others; true leaders esteem others better than themselves.

  Phil. 2.3 *Let nothing be done through selfish ambition or conceit, but in lowliness of mind let each esteem others better than himself.*

- Abusers rely on the power of authority; true leaders rely on the power of servanthood.

  Matt.20.25 *But Jesus called them to Himself and said, "You know that the rulers of the Gentiles lord it over them, and those who are great exercise authority over them.*

- Abusers make service and ministry a grind; true leaders make labor worthwhile.

  The entire book of Nehemiah

- Abusers serve themselves and their goals; true leaders serve others.

  1 Cor. 9:19 *For though I am free from all men, I have made myself a servant to all, that I might win the more.*

- Abusers wield authority; true leaders empower people.

  2 Tim. 2:2 *And the things that you have heard from me among many witnesses, commit these to faithful men who will be able to teach others also.*

- Abusers fix blame; true leaders fix mistakes.

  Philemon 1:18-19 *But if he has wronged you or owes anything, put that on my account. I, Paul, am writing with my own hand. I will repay—not to mention to you that you owe me even your own self besides.*

- Abusers know how; true leaders show how.

  Ex. 18:17 *So Moses' father-in-law said to him, "The thing that you do is not good."*

Oh yeah, you're gonna love this. . .

From his examination of Matthew 23, Ken Blue outlines the following "symptoms of abusive religion" in his book, *Healing Spiritual Abuse:*[10]

- Abusive leaders base their spiritual authority on their position of office rather than on their service to the group. Their style of leadership is authoritarian.

- Leaders in abusive churches often say one thing but do another. Their words and deeds do not match.

- They manipulate people by making them feel guilty for not measuring up spiritually. They lay heavy religious loads on people and make no effort to lift those loads. You know you are in an abusive church if the loads just keep getting heavier.

- Abusive leaders are preoccupied with looking good. They labor to keep up appearance. They stifle any criticism that puts them in a bad light.

- They seek honorific titles and special privileges that elevate them above the group. They promote a class system with themselves at the top.

- Their communication is not straight. Their speech becomes especially vague and confusing when they are defending themselves.

- They major on minor issues to the neglect of the truly important ones. They are conscientious about religious details but neglect God's larger agendas.

Interesting Parallels

In writing this book, I've found it interesting, if not shocking, to discover abusive, manipulative religious leaders share a host of traits common to domestic batterers. (But, when you think about it, isn't the same evil spirit behind all abuse?) According to studies offered by such organizations as the *Project for Victims of Family Abuse and the Crisis Support Network*,[11] domestic abusers are characterized by:

- Controlling and manipulative behavior in relationships;
- Insistence on a "pecking order" with them at the top;
- Demand for rigid rules fortifying their authority;
- Using shame and guilt to buffer control;
- Use privilege and entitlement to maintain status;
- Require unrealistic expectations of you and others;
- Push for hasty decisions and immediate responses;
- Refuse to negotiate or compromise decisions;
- Intolerant of differing views;
- Hypersensitive to criticism;
- Exhibit insatiable ego needs;
- Demonstrate childlike narcissism;
- Unreasonable possessiveness;
- Isolate you from other people, groups and ideas;
- Verbally and psychologically degrade subordinates;
- Blame others for problems;
- Deny personal responsibility for problems;
- Use of coercion and intimidation to gain the advantage.

At this point, it's up to you to draw your own conclusions. But as far as I'm concerned, an abuser is an abuser, in your home or in your Church – physically, mentally or spiritually.

Time to Get Real. . .

1. Define the Greek world "kleros" using scriptural references.

2. Define the Greek word "laos" using scriptural references.

3. Can you identify a time in your life when you held one of the positions talked about in this chapter and found yourself manipulating others?

4. Have you ever been confronted by someone with a concern you were being manipulative? If not, how do you think you would respond if you were? How should you respond?

5. Do you think it's okay for people in leadership to manipulate others if the end result for their manipulation is for Souls anyway?

6. What if your best friend is in the habit of manipulating you and is not aware of it? What do you do then?

Chapter 12

"What Am I Supposed to do About It?"

"What Am I Supposed to do About It?"

Within the Church setting, it's not one abuse that might get you to stand up and say something, but an ongoing occurrence of the abuse. If we confronted those in spiritual authority over us every time we "thought" it was happening, it would be a long dis-satisfying relationship. We'd be listening to every word spoken with doubt and unbelieving hearts and would find ourselves unable to truly trust the people that are around us, those God has placed into our lives. We would become cynical and hard hearted towards those who truly love us and care about us with the purist of intentions. That would be a complete mistake and hinder our walk with God, as well as our impact in the world today.

Instead, I think it's important for the Church to watch for **patterns** of abuse within our spiritual leaders. The longer the pattern continues, the more difficult it will be to change it! So don't wait too long to confront when it becomes apparent. Let the Holy Spirit guide you. You need to say something before you reach that breaking point. For example, a child being bullied in the schoolyard can only put up with it for so long before they snap. We've seen workers in factories, employees on their jobs, even pastors' wives who suddenly "snapped" because of the abuse they had to endure for years.

Famous Movie Quote:

1976 Movie NETWORK[1]

"I want you to get up right now, sit up, go to your windows, open them and stick your head out and yell - 'I'm as mad as hell and I'm not going to take this anymore!' Things have got to change. But first, you've gotta get mad!"

That movie quote is an example of how you do not want to act. You need to do something before it gets that bad. Church, we do not want to wait until we get to that point to speak up. As I stated earlier, all of us have "red flags" raised in our minds and spirits when we get into certain situations. When these red flags are raised, we have to pay attention to them. It's a form of discernment that the Holy Spirit has given us to help us along our journey. It's when we ignore these warnings we get ourselves into trouble. It's when we ignore these flags of distress we get in over our heads and have a difficult time trying to recover. The first thing we must do when feeling like we're being manipulated is to discern whether or not it's happening. We need to spend time in prayer, asking the Holy Spirit to give us a heart of discernment that can only come from Him. Then, if we feel manipulation is taking place, and that God has given us the go ahead, we need to do something about it.

So, what should the Church do when they feel they are being spiritually manipulated?

Allow me to suggest the following. . .

#1: Discern Motivations

A great deal of the time, manipulation can be determined by the motivation of one's heart. For example, is it a Spirit of manipulation that leads me to ask our worship pastor and team to come up at the end of my message? Do I desire to manipulate people into responding to the challenge? Absolutely not. What is motivating me to ask them to play their music is that I want to do everything possible to provide an atmosphere for God to move in one's life. I'm motivated by the desire for the Holy Spirit to move. If we build an atmosphere in which the Holy Spirit can move upon the Church in His own way, then so be it! That should be the motive behind everything we do when we gather together in our respective places of worship.

Does the Holy Spirit need our music? No. Does the Holy Spirit need our words to move? No. However, He does use us as His instruments in providing an atmosphere that is Holy and non-adulterated in a world that is full of idolatry, confusion, manipulation, pride and sin. That's what motivates me.

You may feel like you're being manipulated, but always keep in mind the *motivation* behind the person. Get to know their hearts. Try to spend some time with them and catch their way of thinking - the story behind their lives. If you know their hearts and the motivations behind what they do and say, you may find the appearance of manipulation is actually an expression of a pure heart and desire to see God's Kingdom advanced. They might just be going about it in a wrong way. If that's the case, then you must give them grace and make yourself available to help them along the journey if they so desire.

#2: Stay and Pray

Let's say you know without a doubt you are being manipulated and that God is releasing you to do something about it. With this being the case, you have a few options before you; one of those options is to do nothing but Stay and Pray; to suck it up and stay under their leadership. This may be the most difficult option, especially if you have strong ties to a Church body or group. To remain in a climate of religious control is spiritually repressive, even toxic to your spiritual health and the wellbeing of your family.[2] It can get old quick and you'll want to jump ship as quickly as possible; but if you feel God (and not guilt) requires you to stay, then Stay and Pray. I've learned over the years that the most arduous of situations can change in answer to prayer. Your prayers to the Father, being offered consistently with Faith, can make all the difference in the world! No matter what you're dealing with, it's not too much to ask!

However, you need to know, that in spiritually abusive groups you should usually expect change to come at a snail's pace. Controlling, manipulative spirits will vigorously resist any change that threatens their ennobled office, especially if the leader they are influencing feels their position is scriptural or has been learned through training and upbringing. It may take a while for you to see the change take place, thus it's the most difficult of options - to stay.

But if you decide to stay, do not stay to fillet the church, its leader, or members. Do not stay to criticize, tear open, abuse, or "dog" on the people. It is best to leave the matter in God's hands altogether, or to leave that particular Church family altogether. To stay in a contentious situation to fight usually proves to be counterproductive, especially in an unhealthy environment of control, and does little good. If you have asked God to change the situation, allow Him to do so . . . without your help! Complaining and criticizing may give you a false sense of management over the crisis — at least you are doing something, right? — But it is a feeble and usually ineffectual way of striking back at your problem, especially in abusively controlling relationships.

I've seen first hand, people in a Church who have disagreed with leadership and considered them to be manipulative; stay and attempt to see them "set free". But during their attempts to see this happen, they caused more harm to themselves, their families, and the entire Body of Christ than they would have if they had just left.

For Pete's sake, if you feel you must stay, I whole-heartedly recommend, in these instances, you seek wise counsel from an objective, Biblically-knowledgeable and spiritually-grounded pastor, friend, or professional counselor. It is best to find someone outside your group or denomination. Openly and honestly share the problem from your perspective and listen, and be prepared to follow their advice. If they confirm you are to stay, then stay and pray. But if they don't, then consider the next option.

#3: Confront

If you see a fault in a brother and do nothing about it, you really can't complain about that fault. For some people, how will they know they are manipulating if no one ever tells them? I suggest you talk to the person who you feel has been spiritually abusing you through manipulation. If you don't, how will they know? And how will they ever make a decision to change? You risk the chance they might say you are out of order or that you are wrong. You run the risk of losing a friendship. But you have to do it. Remember, it is the Truth that sets us free. If they are manipulating you, speak the Truth. Then, the possibilities of them being set free will greatly increase.

Famous Movie Quote:

1993 Movie SCHINDLER'S LIST[3]

Amon Goeth speaking to Helen: *"The truth, Helen, is always the right answer."*

By all means, if you've been offended by your brother or sister, you have no choice but to talk to them and get it worked out to the best of your ability. The manner in which you do this must be according to Matthew 18:15-17 (NKJV) *Moreover if your brother sins against you, go and tell him his fault between you and him alone. If he hears you, you have gained your brother. But if he will not hear, take with you one or two more, that by the mouth of two or three witnesses every word may be established. And if he refuses to hear them, tell it to the church. But if he refuses even to hear the church, let him be to you like a heathen and a tax collector.*

Notice the word "brother" in verse 15. This is addressed to Christians. This is dealing with believers who are in conflict.

This reminds me of the Peanuts Comic Strip by Charles Schulz: Lucy demands Linus change TV channels and threatens him with her fist if he doesn't.

Famous Cartoon Quote:

Peanuts Comic Strip by Charles Schulz[4]
Linus: *"What makes you think you can walk right in here and take over?"*

> Lucy: *"These five fingers. Individually they're nothing but when I curl them together like this into a single unit, they form a weapon that is terrible to behold."*
>
> Linus: *"Which channel do you want?"*
>
> [Turning away, he looks at his fingers]
>
> Linus: *"Why can't you guys get organized like that?"*

Remember, we are *The Church*. We are a number of individuals who have a relationship with Jesus Christ, who is the Head of who we are; our Father. We are a family. You and I are connected in covenant relationship with one another through Jesus. Our connection with the Father affects and governs our relationships with each other, and our relationships with each other affects our relationship with God.

It is so important you and I have a right relationship with each other. Jesus addressed this matter in Matthew 5:23-24. *Jesus said, "Therefore, if you are offering your gift at the altar and there remember that your brother has something against you, leave your gift there in front of the altar. First go and be reconciled to your brother; then come and offer your gift."* In fact, the last thing Jesus prayed for His Church was that the Father would make us one, as Jesus is one with the Father!

Author, Dr. Larry Crabb wrote, "The difference between spiritual and unspiritual community is not whether conflict exists, but is rather in our attitude toward it and our approach to handling it. When conflict is seen as an opportunity to draw more fully on spiritual resources, we have the makings of spiritual community."[5] In other words, it is how we handle conflict that determines the level of our spiritual maturity! I love it. Dr. Crabb has crystalized the very heart of what reconciliation can be about.

The truth of the matter is that relationships can be strengthened through conflict if we handle them correctly. **What makes or breaks relationships and what makes or breaks Churches, is what they choose to do in conflict.** We must learn how to walk in love while dealing with conflict. We must have the right attitude.

At the beginning of Matthew 18, Jesus sets the stage for His teaching on conflict resolution by saying this: (v.3-4) *We are to become as little children.* Granted, we've all seen Christians act like little children when it comes to getting their way, but that is not what Jesus is talking about. Verse 4 is the key: *We are to humble ourselves like a little child.*

Along with having the right attitude, it is of incredible importance we walk in humility.[6] To be humble means to bring low. And that is the opposite of what the flesh wants to do in conflict. Flesh seeks to exalt itself, to justify itself, to prove itself right. If that is how we approach a conflict, the conflict will only grow. I can remember times when I thought I had been wronged; a part of me wanted to lash out and strike against the person who hurt me with words that would cut them to the quick. I was angry and wanted them to know it. Thankfully, the Holy Spirit reminded me about walking with a heart of humility.

When we are dealing with conflict with another person, **the goal is reconciliation**, not justification. In other words, our hope is to mend the relationship, not to choose sides and declare a winner. If only one person wins, everybody loses. We must ask the Lord to search our hearts before we ever deal with a conflict. We must ask ourselves, "Am I walking in - and motivated by - love?" If not, get your heart right first, and then deal with the problem at hand.

Love, love, love, love, love

Through the text of Matthew 18, Jesus gives us a very simple four-step plan on how to handle conflict. I suggest you use this four-step approach when confronting those who have abused, controlled, or manipulated you. We make things so complicated, but Jesus makes it simple. If you enter the offices of Eastgate Community Church you'll see a sign on the wall that says, "*Keep It Simple*." That has become one of our goals. And as you confront, keep it simple.

The scriptural way to start is to have a private conversation with the one whom you have the conflict. This is where we most often miss it right off the bat! What does He say to do? *Go to the person who has sinned against you!* This means we do not go to our friends, our Church family, our neighbors, our family, our best friend, our friends on Facebook[7], or any other type of social networking, but rather to the person with whom there is a problem. If someone comes to you with a problem about another person, here is what you need to ask him or her. "Have you addressed this with that person?" If not, encourage them to do so. That is where Jesus said to start.

Ford Taylor has a unique way to get people in conflict to talk to each other. When someone tries to share with him a problem they have with someone else, he'll take out his cell phone (in the midst of the conversation, mind you) and continue to behave as if he's paying attention. He'll then open up the phone and begin scrolling through his contact list to find a number. He'll put his finger on the "send" button without actually pushing it as he stops you from talking and says, "Just one minute. I've got such and such's number and ready to push send if you want to talk to them right now. This isn't an issue we should be talking about together without him in the room, so how about I make the call so you can tell him directly?" That usually stops the conversation right then. I tell this to the people in our Church family; if they are planning to come to me about a conflict with another person, I can save them some time. There's no need to talk to me, so don't make the appointment. Talk to the person you have conflict with first. I can't help them if you're not willing to address the issue with them first.

When you need to have a private conversation with somebody, let me encourage you to do it as quickly as you can. Don't put off the conflict for weeks or months hoping it will go away. It won't. You've been dealing with this manipulative spirit for a long time and it isn't just going to go away for no reason. In fact, it will more than likely only get worse as anger and bitterness take root in your soul. At the same time, the offense tends to get blown out of proportion the longer it sits unaddressed. Remember what Jesus said about leaving your gift at the altar. The reason it is so urgent to the Lord is because of the damage it can create if gone untreated. If we had a broken arm, wouldn't we want the injury repaired as soon as possible? Offenses are far more devastating to the soul and spirit, and eventually to the Body of Christ, than a broken arm.

Face-to-Face is Always Better!

When you meet, make sure you have spent a great amount of time in quality prayer, asking God for favor, wisdom, and clarity as you speak. Believe Him that all walls of lies and deceit will be bound and that the person you will be confronting will have an open heart and spirit to listen to you. Remember, this is a spiritual battle and that person is not your enemy; the devil is. *The person who has been controlling and abusing you with manipulation is not and will not ever be your enemy.* This is a spirit far more sinister than the person being used by it. That is why it is of importance that you spend quality time with God in advance of the meeting. Asking for His protection, strength, favor, and anointing to be manifest during your confrontation will be the key to the success of true freedom.

After this has been done, plan to meet face-to-face. Jesus said, *"Go and show him his fault."* That means no e-mail, no phone call, no text, no letter, or note. With as many electronic means we have to communicate today, nothing is better than looking them in the eye and dealing with the issue, eye-to-eye, heart-to-heart. Anything less than a face-to-face conversation places a barrier between the people involved. Then, when you are together, start by genuinely affirming the relationship. Let the person know you are seeking to resolve the conflict, not to assign blame. Let the person know up front how much they mean to you. Be genuine in your care and love for them. Take the time to let them know your love for them is real and you really do value your relationship. This person has been in some type of leadership role over you, so be respectful of that position and honor them for being who they are. If it's your pastor, or a board member, or any of the other people to whom I referred in the previous chapters, make sure you go with the greatest of intent of showing them you love them. Don't be manipulative yourself, just walk with love.

As the meeting progresses, make sure you make *observations* and not *accusations*. That means addressing actions that have occurred, rather than pointing a finger or attacking their character. My bride Butch is always reminding me to use "I" statements instead of "you" statements when I'm in this type of situation. "I feel that you did me wrong" is better than, "You are a liar! You don't care about anyone but yourself!" Address what you have seen or perceived and felt. Don't accuse and put them on the defensive. Take ownership of your feelings. Putting them on the defensive is only going to create even higher walls and the spirit of manipulation (that is already at play) is more than likely going to get even more elevated. There is no need to do this.

As you are going into the meeting, make sure you have the facts about why it is you feel they are being manipulative and controlling. Share with them certain times, dates, and things they have said that have made you feel the way you do. Do not give them generalizations, but give them actual times so they can reflect and remember. Give them actual events and statements that they have made, be specific and clear. Remember not to lump everyone else in with your accusations. You are not there to speak on behalf of anyone else except for yourself. You don't say things like, "A lot of us have been feeling. . ." If others are feeling that way, then they need to speak on behalf of themselves. You just speak for yourself.

After you make your observations and state your facts, allow the other person to respond. There may be things you have not been aware of or have misunderstood. This might be the time you come to the realization that their motives have actually been pure; they have just gone about it in the wrong way. Praise God if that is the case! This then will give you an opportunity to move forward with a game plan to help each of you understand more clearly your intentions and bring unity to not only yourselves, but possibly to the entire Body of Christ also dealing with this. You want to promote resolution. The point is not to fight, win, or prove them wrong. The point is to restore trust and harmony so that you can be a healthy member of the Church along with this person, who is among those you consider your spiritual authority.

Please remember that a person who is dealing with a spirit of manipulation may or may not accept the truth of what you are trying to say. That spirit is heavy duty and it will more often than not take more than just one conversation to get things resolved. Be prepared for them to tell you that you are "out of line," or how dare you "touch the hand of God's anointed." Be prepared to be labeled as an outcast. Be prepared to take some "heat" for speaking out about what you believe to be true. And more than likely it may be spoken about in public, as opposed to private (as you have done in setting up the meeting with them).

That is why you must be dedicated in advance to prayer, using the wisdom given to you by God to come against that evil spirit. Remember, you are not coming against the person, but the spirit. And, if by the grace of God you are successful in showing them the reality of their abuse, then all the Glory to God! But what if they don't see it? What do you do if they are obstinate? What if they refuse to discuss it or don't want to make the relationship right and come clean of his or her manipulative ways? Then you have no choice but to go to the next step according to God's Word, and take a witness with you.

These witnesses are there for the same reason; to bring reconciliation. It is not to gang up on the person! In fact, we should involve others only when going alone did not bring a healing. What are we talking about? A mediator. A neutral person. Someone who can help keep emotions in check and help clarify the issues.

Be Careful Church

If that doesn't bring resolution, then the next step comes into the picture. The third step is the most drastic. Take it to the Church.

This is a tough one in some cases, because the one who is manipulating may be your pastor, your Sunday school teacher, your elder, your worship leader, etc. What do you do when the person who is causing the harm *is* the spiritual authority?

First of all, get this in your mind: it's not your job to set them free! It is not your responsibility to make sure that person changes his or her ways and walks in deliverance from the evil Spirit of manipulation and control. That is God's job. The situation you are in right now is a personal, one-on-one situation you are responsible to try and resolve. You are not a "spokesperson" for the Church; you are just one member of the Church. It is not the entire Church against the authority. It is you, the individual Church member, who has a problem with this person in authority; thus you handle it with Holy Spirit "kid gloves" with the intent of not bringing division or harm to the Church, the Body of Christ. It's a personal issue between the two of you.

It is my suggestion at this point you tell the person who has offended you through manipulation and control that you would like to set up a meeting with him or her and the people to whom they are personally accountable. These individuals could include a board of elders, core leadership, staff, parish, or whomever they may be accountable. Talk with this group. But <u>do not do it behind their back</u>. You simply tell them you want to have a meeting to discuss with them your concerns and keep it as private as you can. You should do everything you can to protect the reputation of the spiritual authority with whom you have the problem.

What if you're wrong?

Let me ask you; what if you are wrong? What if the claims and accusations of manipulation and control you are making are wrong? What if the facts come back and it turns out you are the one in the wrong? Then what? Then you've got to repent and come clean yourself! You've got to repent to the Father of the Bride and then repent to your spiritual authority, along with anyone else you may have infected with your thoughts and accusations, and make it right. It would be a good idea for you to take some time off of any type of public ministry where you represent the Church in any type of leadership role, submit yourself to your spiritual authority, and wait for their counsel as to the next steps you should take. You've got to learn from this experience and allow the Holy Spirit to speak to your heart as you let the wounds heal.

If you go about trying to stain the reputation of those in authority over you and begin to actually touch the hand of God's anointed, woe be unto you. Remember, the overall goal is reconciliation, whether you are wrong or they are wrong. So you ask in all humility to set up the meeting. If that person genuinely feels they are innocent and willing to work this out, they will have no problem making the meeting happen. However, if they are guilty and the Spirit of manipulation rises up, there is no way they'll want to have this meeting. If that is the case, you walk away.

Some conflicts will not be resolved. The last step is to break off the relationship and walk away. If you cannot reach an agreement or even agree to disagree, then separation is called for. Jesus said to *treat them as a pagan or tax collector*. Does that mean treat them like scoundrels? No. Jesus loved pagans and tax collectors. He walked in love with them in the hope of winning them over.

Romans 12:18. *"If it is possible"* indicates that it may not be. *"As far as it depends on you"* means that you only have to do your part, *"live at peace"* is the goal for how you are to live.

If you have someone who refuses to be reconciled with you, ask yourself these questions, "Do I long to be reconciled?" "Do I still act in love toward this person?" If so, then you are doing your part. It is now up to the other person.

Right after this teaching, Peter asks Jesus about forgiving others. That is an important key for you in moving forward. Forgiveness. We have been forgiven much by God, and therefore we must forgive others who wrong us. They may never admit to the wrong, but you forgive them anyway. They may bad mouth you and stain your reputation, but you forgive them anyway. They may never want anything to do with you and try to make life miserable for you and your family. If they do, you *still* have to forgive them.

Remember, the truth will always win in every circumstance. You do not have to defend yourselves in these matters. Let the Holy Spirit defend you in His time, and in His way. You just be you and move on.

It is said that Leonardo da Vinci, when painting the Last Supper, painted Judas' face as the face of someone with whom he was angry. But he found that he could not paint the face of Jesus until he changed the face of Judas. Remember the Lord's Prayer: *"Forgive us our sins, as we forgive those who sin against us."*

#4: Feel free to walk away quietly

In certain situations, this is the best thing to do. Just walk away. This will be difficult; however, if you've been with a Church family for a long period of time. The longer you've been with that family the tougher it will be to walk away. In some cases when you are really not plugged into the body, just walk away. Do not make a big fuss over it by talking to others, which will lead to division, just walk away quietly and go somewhere where you feel comfortable. Allow the Lord to heal and restore you spiritually.

If you go, please do it the right way. You should never leave with a vindictive desire to get back at those who hurt you. You should never leave with unforgiveness in your heart, as I stated previously. You should never leave with the intent to stir up trouble on the way out the door. You should never leave with bitterness in your heart. And, you should never leave in pride or thinking you are better than anyone else.

Leaving a church or organization is a difficult decision to make, especially when you have strong bonds and friendships within the group. Your friends will resist your decision to leave their fellowship. Many will want to know why you are leaving and expect the "honest and dirty truth." Others may brand you as a troublemaker (or worse) and accuse you of abandoning them. But, you need to know the Bible supports, and even encourages, your decision to flee from spiritually abusive and oppressive situations.

Romans 16:17-18 (NKJV) *Now I urge you, brethren, note those who cause divisions and offenses, contrary to the doctrine which you learned, and avoid them. For those who are such do not serve our Lord Jesus Christ, but their own belly, and by smooth words and flattering speech deceive the hearts of the simple.*

Colossians 2:4 (NKJV) *Now this I say lest anyone should deceive you with persuasive words.*

2 Tim.2:14-16 (NKJV) *Remind them of these things, charging them before the Lord not to strive about words to no profit, to the ruin of the hearers. Be diligent to present yourself approved to God,*

a worker who does not need to be ashamed, rightly dividing the word of truth. But shun profane and idle babblings, for they will increase to more ungodliness.

Jesus made it very clear to His generation that they were not to trust, nor submit to the oppressive control of the Pharisees.

This point is big and really important!

However and please hear my heart, if you leave, do not abandon your faith in Jesus Christ! Do not allow yourself to become one of those who becomes so disenfranchised with the modern day Church that you want nothing to do with it. Avoid the temptation to become a casualty by dropping-out. Before leaving a spiritually malignant group, seek and follow the advice of a Godly Christian leader who can advise you impartially. Simply running away from a problem is no solution, especially if you have no direction in which to flee. Locate a fellowship based on true scriptural servant-leadership, mutual respect, and love for one another, whose priorities and leadership follow the model of Jesus Christ, and whose teachings are sound. They're out there! Don't give up on the Body of Christ – The Church. The Church needs you. The Church is the people – and you are an important part of that Church! Yes, leave the place you are currently attending. **But do not give up on God or His Church!**

REMEMBER, you'll find no perfect Church. The reason is because the Church is the people, and people sin! Until Jesus comes back for His Bride, the Church, we will all be growing and per-fecting ourselves in the ways of the Father. No matter where you go, there will be controlling, manipulative spirits with whom you will have to deal. The enemy will see to it! If it is a situation where you are being manipulated through a television program or other type of ministry, just turn it off, walk away, and stop watching it. But don't give up on The Church!

#5: Be Respectful

For most of us, the ones in our Churches who have had a tendency to manipulate over the years are our spiritual fathers and mothers. These are hand-picked individuals who God has placed in our lives to mentor and disciple us. Why would we not be respectful? The moment you show a lack of respect for them, you miss out on being the example of Christ in love and character. Respect is a must!

You have no right to speak down to them in a condescending way. You have no right to speak in a judgmental way either to their face or behind their back. You have no right to let your flesh get the better of you. You must have a heart of love and absolute respect for their position. If you don't respect their position, you shouldn't expect to be respected either. Respect is a two way street; you give it, you get it back. If you disrespect others, you can count on being disrespected also.

Matthew 19:19 (ESV) *Honor your father and mother, and, You shall love your neighbor as yourself.*

#6: Leave Your Judgmental Attitude at Home

Refrain from becoming judgmental towards your leadership. For the most part, your leaders have loved you and want nothing but God's absolute best for your life. When it comes right down to it, I believe they do love you. They do care about you. They do want God's best for you. But remember, they are only human and fall into the same traps that everyone else does. Remember, we only have one enemy, and it's not them. Sometimes we expect our leaders to walk on water. We expect them to eat manna and follow glory clouds by day and flashes of fire by night! They are going to blow it. I guarantee it. So give them the grace given to everyone else and keep loving and praying for them. Show your respect and support for whom they are and the role they play in your life.

Time to Get Real. . .

1. Have you ever left a Church before? What were the reasons for you leaving? Did you have the blessings of the leadership to go?
2. Have you ever become bitter against the Church?
3. What six steps should be followed when you feel you are being spiritually manipulated?
4. Have you given up on the Church?
5. Do you think there is hope for the modern day Church?

6. Have you ever been wrong in your assumptions about someone else? How did you handle that situation?

Is there hope? YES! May you soul draw strength as you read this poem. . .

My Very Heart Betrays Me [8]

By Linzi LaRai Campfield

Dark fancies dance around in my head,
Gliding themselves towards my hands and lips.
My very heart betrays me.
For in my inmost being I long to be pure,
To be free of the wretched desires that grasp around me.
But their sweet siren sound pierces my ears
With lies that ring as truth,
Only, when finished, to leave me in despair and want, yet again.
But I am tired of wickedness.
And I am sick of the sorrow that plagues my mind.
I may feel too weak to defeat this
And I may have crashed and fallen in my own fight,
But the One who loves me is far stronger than any beast that vies
for my heart.
He will vanquish the evil that surrounds me with but a raise of His
mighty hand

And He will raise me up and bring me peace once again.

No longer will temptation consume me.

And no longer will I fear in the night,

But I will "submit to God and be at peace with Him,

And in this way, prosperity will come." (Job 22:21)

"This Book is Nearing Its Conclusion"

Ahhhhhhhh

Conclusion

*T*he late great Presbyterian clergyman, musician, and hymn writer, Rev. Maltbie Davenport Babcock (1858 - 1901), once said, *"Christianity is not a voice in the wilderness, but a life in the world. It is not an idea in the air but feet on the ground, going God's way. It is not an exotic flower to be kept under glass, but a hardy plant to bear twelve months of fruits in all kinds of weather. Fidelity to duty is its root and branch. Nothing we can say to the Lord, no calling Him by great or dear names, can take the place of the plain doing of His will. We may cry out about the beauty of eating bread with Him in His Kingdom, but it is wasted breath and a rootless hope, unless we plow and plant in His Kingdom here and now. To remember Him at His Table and to forget Him at ours is to have invested in bad securities. There is no substitute for plain, every-day goodness."* [1]

A very fine line exists between the healthy and unhealthy use of power! At any point in time, even the best of leaders can begin making decisions that increasingly place their own interests before the needs of others, thus becoming manipulators. And as you've seen, such misuse of power is not always subtle either! History tells the stories of numerous leaders who boldly acted as if their position placed them above "real accountability."

Yes, there are and always will be those in the Church that will manipulate others for their own gain. Yes, there are and always will be those in the Body of Christ who will abuse others, knowingly or not. It's not going to change. But what can change is the Church standing up and saying, "No More!" What can, and must change, is the Body of Christ drawing a line in the sand, taking the heart of a servant and not allowing themselves to be abused.

So, with all of this manipulation taking place over the years in the Church, how is it that God has been able to move in such powerful ways? I'll tell you why; it's called GRACE! It's only by God's grace that we are where we are. And just think where the Church would be if we didn't have all of this manipulation going on? We would be way above the realities to where we are now in our IMPACT for God in our world.

The good news is, the Church is coming alive to Truth! The spiritual leaders are beginning to lead in Truth! The Church is becoming what God has called us to be: free from sin, non-manipulating family members who love each other and desire to live and work together in harmony to make an IMPACT for Jesus Christ, to change the culture that we each live in!

Church, Stop Being Manipulated!

And as you do. . . You watch, you wait, you'll see!

For Your Benefit. . .

At the end of each chapter I present a series of questions under the heading *"Time to Get Real."* This is your opportunity to *"get real"* in dealing with your own issues of spiritual manipulation. There are a number of ways to ensure this exercise will be the most impactful for your life. Of course, you can answer the questions on your own, which is good; but in order to get the greater impact, I would suggest that you *"get real"* in the midst of a small group of people within your own Church family.

If you are a person in a leadership role within the Body of Christ, spiritually manipulating people, you might want to get together with a group of fellow manipulators and call it a *"Spiritual Manipulators Support Group."*

Ford Taylor, once told me that in every relationship we have we need to have four things. If we live by these four things with each other, nothing can stop us from doing what God has destined for our lives. I believe if you will adopt these in your small group experience it will greatly enhance your quest for freedom of spiritual manipulation.

<u>Consider adapting the following guidelines as you meet together. . .</u>

(1) *Pre-forgiveness.* We need to forgive each other even before we hurt each other. The fact is we are going to hurt each other. We

296

are going to cause harm to each other because we are human. We need to live a life of pre-forgiveness; which means, I forgive you even before you hurt me. There may be things said in the group you won't agree with and might take personally. Someone may express something that offends your heart; it happens. In reality, not only does it happen, but it more than likely *will* happen if each of you are being truly honest with each other. Be so in love with each other that you have pre-forgiveness.

(2) *Humility*. We must have humility in our lives with each other. Pride will kill and destroy any relationship. As the Bible says in Proverbs 16:18, *"Pride comes first, then the fall."* With your desire for humility in your small group, humility would encourage you to be respectful of each other's time. Don't hog the conversation and make it all about you. Don't allow your "troubles" to take the group hostage, making it difficult for others to give their opinions and share their hearts. Don't allow your pride to manipulate the group and conversation that takes place.

(3) *Unconditional Love*. Our love for each other should not be conditional. We cannot base our love for each other upon the actions or responses of others. I do not love you because of what you do for me; I love you because of who you are. We cannot place conditions on our love for each other. And because we love

297

each other and the Body of Christ, we chose to not spread gossip or talk about others by naming names that may bring hurt, confusion, and strife. In our conversations, we need to bless those who have hurt us, spiritually abused us, or caused us harm. Love is a must whether that person is sitting in the room or not.

(4) *100% Truth*. We must be able to speak the truth to each other. If we hide the truth, we will be unable to truly deal with issues and have true peace with each other. My father, Rev. Jerral Campfield, has always taught me that we need to be transparent with people, meaning that we need to be real. We all wear masks from time to time. We try to hide our mistakes, our faults, our sins, and our insecurities. We wear masks so often, at times they seem as if they are a reality to us. Friends, take off the masks in your life and be real. God genuinely loves you and He desires others love you, too. However, how can they if you are always wearing a mask? Take off the mask. Be real. Allow your small group experience to be one of Truth.

Guidelines for Leaders

Every group needs a leader. Once the leader is selected or agreed upon, consider the following guidelines to help make your small group experience one of greater impact.

Exemplify the Four Guidelines Above — If you are not being an example of pre-forgiveness, humility, unconditional love, and 100% Truth you cannot expect your small group to do the same.

Pray — Before the group comes together, take some time to pray; asking the Holy Spirit to have His way in the meeting; that He will accomplish what He has in store in your time together. Remember, you only have one enemy and it is not man; it's the devil. And the devil will do everything he can to keep the Body of Christ in a manipulative state. Prayer is a must in this spiritual battle.

Interruptions — There will always be someone who breaks in while another person is speaking. Most interrupting during discussion is due to enthusiasm rather than rudeness. Control the interruptions by saying things like, "Hold that thought, Cathi. We'll want to hear it again once Dave has finished."

Monopolizing Conversation — Don't allow anyone to monopolize the conversation. Come up with a game plan before you meet with how you will handle this. The fact is, as it is happening, usually everyone in the room is aware of the monopolizing, except for the monopolizer! In the Focus Group I had in preparing this book, I put a bell in the middle of the table that anyone could ring if they felt like the person talking was going too long. We made it fun. As well, you can cut in on a longwinded group member with, "That's an interesting point you just made Max. Did anyone else get the same impression or a different one?" "You've made some interesting points, Cazi. Let's hear from another reader. Linzi? What did you think?"

Keeping the group on the topic of the book — It's important that you allow the Holy Spirit to lead your discussion, to accomplish what He desires each time you meet. Don't be afraid to get "off topic" if the Spirit is leading the group in that direction; but try not to let members wander too far off subject. Bring them back if they do. Comments such as, "Let's get back to the question hand. What did you think at this point?" "I have a question about the situation on page 125. What's really happening here?"

Listen carefully to what is said by participants — Don't let your mind wander. Stay connected with the group. Rephrase a reader's comments or question to be sure you and others understand what was meant. This is an especially necessary technique when dealing with a long-winded participant.

Allow everyone the chance to contribute to the discussion — Engage silent readers by posing open-ended questions directly. But don't badger the participants who really don't want to participate. They may not have finished that chapter of the book and don't want to admit it.

Remind everyone of the next meeting time and chapter to be discussed — It's great to have the meeting at the same place and time each gathering for the sake of familiarity and ease, but you may want to switch it up. Either way, make sure your group knows the plan in moving forward.

Be brief — As facilitator, your comments and segues should be brief, and you should not speak more than anyone else in the dialogue. Do not talk after each person has spoken. Do not encourage participants to direct all comments towards you. The meeting should not be about you!

No gossip — As facilitator, one of your responsibilities is to make sure that the small group meeting doesn't become a place where members can "air someone's dirty laundry." It is not a place to talk about how displeased we are with our spiritual authority and talk behind their backs. No names should be mentioned when dealing with people who are not in the room. Do not hide the fact that you are meeting as a group from your spiritual authority. *Invite them to join you!* The facilitator cannot allow one negative word to come out that may bring strife, dissention, discord, hurt feelings, or negativity. And if it happens, the facilitator must deal with it quickly, not allowing it to get "out of hand." If the group finds that the facilitator is the one bringing the harm, then he/she must be dealt with quickly according to Matthew 18.

Have fun! — The topic of spiritual abuse can be extremely heavy, simply because it is truly a heavy subject! But that doesn't mean that you can't have fun together as a group. Enjoy the process. Try to bring in levity when it gets too heavy. Think of some experiences you've had in the past that might bring a lighter spirit to the meeting. Be serious when you need to be – but have fun doing it.

Special Thanks...

In working on this project, I felt impressed by the Holy Spirit to form a "FOCUS GROUP." A **focus group** is a form of qualitative research in which a group of people are asked about their perceptions, opinions, beliefs, and attitudes towards a product, service, concept, advertisement, idea, or packaging.

Questions are asked in an interactive group setting where participants are free to talk with other group members.

I was blessed to have the following denominational backgrounds represented in this Focus Group that brought great insight from each of their perspective backgrounds.

Lutheran, Baptist, Assembly of God, Catholic, Apostolic, African American Methodist, Presbyterian, Open Bible, Non-denominational, Southern Baptist, Church of God, Former Atheist, Nazarene, United Methodist.

Members of this quality group of Christ Followers consisted of...

Joe Arthur

Joe Kresser

Sue Polaski

Sharan Strub

David and Arlene Schleppi

Marc and Therese Bell

Flint and Alicia McCallum

Dixie Dixon

Brandon Pierce

A huge thanks to all of you! I could not have done this without you!

Notes

Introduction

1. http://www.sermoncentral.com, *Recognizing and Recovering From Spiritual Abuse*, Jim Miller, 2003.

2. Zig Ziglar, *The Ziglar Weekly Newsletter*, July 20, 2010, Edition #29.

3. Frank Viola, George Barna, *Pagan Christianity: Exploring the Roots of Our Church Practices*, Tyndale House, 2008.

4. Frank Viola, George Barna, *Pagan Christianity: Exploring the Roots of Our Church Practices*, Tyndale House, 2008.

5. http://www.wikipedia.com

6. http://www.dalecampfield.com, *Hey God, Is It Too Much to Ask?*, Xulon Press, 2012.

Chapter One

1. http://www.imdb.com, Memorable Movie Quotes, The Lord of the Rings: Return of the King, New Line Cinema, Time Warner, 2003.

Chapter Two

1. http://www.imdb.com, Memorable Movie Quotes, Toy Story 3, Pixar Animation Studios, 2010.

Chapter Three

1. http://www.imdb.com, Memorable Movie Quotes, Thor, Paramount Pictures, 2011.
2. http://www.imdb.com, Memorable Movie Quotes, Star Wars: A New Hope, George Lucas, 1977.
3. http://www.imdb.com, Memorable Movie Quotes, Groundhog Day, Harold Ramis, 1993.

Chapter Four

1. http://www.sermoncentral.com, *Recognizing and Recovering From Spiritual Abuse*, Jim Miller, 2003.

Chapter Five

1. Joseph Mattera, *Ruling In the Gates: Preparing the Church to Transform Cities*, 2003; *Walk in Generational Blessings: Leaving a Legacy of Transformation Through Your Family*, 2012; *Kingdom Revolution: Bringing Change to Your Life and Beyond*, 2009; *Kingdom Awakening*, 2010.

2. Zig Ziglar, *The Ziglar Weekly Newsletter*, July 20, 2010, Edition #29.

3. http://www.imdb.com, Memorable Movie Quotes, Back to the Future, Universal Studios, 1985.

4. http://www.imdb.com, Memorable Movie Quotes, The King's Speech, Tom Hooper, David Seidler, 2010.

5. Zig Ziglar, *The Ziglar Weekly Newsletter*, July 20, 2010, Edition #29.

Chapter Six

1. Os Hillman, *The Religious Spirit and Spiritual Strongholds in the Workplace*, Article, 2013.

2. Dr. C. Peter Wagner, *Freedom From the Religious Spirit*, Regal Books, 2005.

3. Dr. C. Peter Wagner, *Freedom From the Religious Spirit*, Regal Books, 2005.

4. http://www.wen.wikipedia.org/wiki/Martin_Luther, Martin Luther, 2013.

5. Rick Joyner, *Combating the Religious Spirit*, Morning Star Publications, Chapter 7, *Epic Battles of the Last Days*, 2012.

6. http://www.angelfire.com, *4 Major Characteristics of a Religious Spirit*, 1997. http://www.cbn.com, *The Warning Signs of Toxic Religion*, J. Lee Grady, 2013; http://www.m.youversion.com, *How To Recognize the Religious Spirit Part II*, 2011; Jonas Clark, *30 Pieces of Silver: Jesus Opposes what the Religious Spirit is Doing*, Spirit Life ministries, 2004.

7. http://www.memidex.com/gossippings, Memidex Free Online Dictionary, 2013.

8. http://www.facebook.com, Social Media Website, 2013.

9. http://www.imdb.com, Memorable Movie Quotes, School of Rock, Richard Linklater, Mike White, 2003.

10 Os Hillman, *The Religious Spirit*, http://www.openheaven.com, 2005; Dr. C. Peter Wagner, *Freedom From the Religious Spirit*, Regal Books, 2005.

11 http://www.truthinreality.com, *Prayer of Release From a Religious Spirit*, 2013.

Chapter Seven

1. http://www.sermoncentral.com, *Keys to Spiritual Authority*, Bruce Morrison, 2003.

Chapter Eight

1. Ingrid Hansen, *Fighting the Spirit of Manipulation: Going Deeper, Growing Higher*, 2011.
2. http://www.imdb.com, Memorable Movie Quotes, Monty Python and the Holy Grail, Monty Python, 1975.
3. *JOY*, Words and Music by Bud Metzger and Sally Lewis, Date Unknown.
4. http://www.imdb.com, Memorable Movie Quotes, The Wizard of Oz, Metro-Golden-Mayer, 1939.
5. http://www.merriam-webster.com_manipulation, 2013.

Chapter Nine

1. http://www.heavenawaits.wordpress.com, *Identify and Destroy the Jezebel Spirit, Sex, Church, Witchcraft*, 2012.
2. http://www.ronnie-outlovesjesus.com, *With God All Things Are Possible: The Jezebel Spirit and How to Slay Her*, 2013.

Chapter Ten

1. http://www.imdb.com, Memorable Movie Quotes, Raiders of the Lost Ark, Steven Spielberg, George Lucas, 1981.

2. Linzi Campfield, *The Strength to Overcome*, 2012.

3. http://www.imdb.com, Memorable Movie Quotes, The Matrix, Larry and Andy Wachowski, 1999.

4. http://www.sermoncentral.com, *Satan's Just Doing His Job*, 2002.

Chapter Eleven

1. http://www.imdb.com, Memorable Movie Quotes, Thor, Paramount Pictures, 2011.

2. http://www.plymouthbrethern.com, Stephen Hesterman, *The Distinction Between Clergy and Laity: Is It of God?*, 2013.

3. Charles Jacobs, *The Story of the Church*, Goodreads, 2012.

4. http://www.imdb.com, Memorable Movie Quotes, Thor, Paramount Pictures, 2011.

5. http://www.haventoday.org/billygrahamsstory.php, Billy Graham's Life Story, 2013.

6. http://www.imdb.com, Memorable Movie Quotes, The Amazing Spiderman, Marc Web, Marvel Comics, 2012.

7. Brennan Manning, *The Ragamuffin Gospel*, Harper One, 2005.

8. http://www.imdb.com, Memorable Movie Quotes, Spiderman, Sam Raimi, Kavid Koepp, Marvel Comics, 2002.

9. http://www.spiritual-journal.blogspot.com, *Spiritual Abuse in Korean Church and Authoritarian Pastors*, 2011.

10 Ken Blue, *Healing Spiritual Abuse: How To Break Free From Bad Church Experiences*, Intervarsity Press, 1993.

11 http://www.supportnetwork.org, *Project for Victims of Family Abuse and the Crisis Support Network*, A Department of the YWCA, 2013.

Chapter Twelve

1. http://www.imdb.com, Memorable Movie Quotes, Network, Metro-Goldwyn-Mayer, 1976.

2. http://www.sermoncentral.com, *Recognizing and Recovering From Spiritual Abuse*, Jim Miller, 2003.

3. http://www.imdb.com, Memorable Movie Quotes, Schindler's List, Steven Spielberg, 1993.

4. http://www.sermonillustrations.com, *Unity*, Charles Schultz, 2012

5. Dr. Larry Crabb, *Becoming a True Spiritual Community: A Profound Vision of What the Church Can Be*, T. Nelson, 1999.

6. http://www.sermoncentral.com, *Dealing with Conflict While Walking in Love*, Chad Payne, 2002.

7. http://www.facebook.com, Social Media Website, 2013.

8. Linzi Campfield, *My Very Heart Betrays Me*, 2012.

Conclusion

1. Maltbie Davenport Babcock, A Reminiscent Sketch and Memorial by Charles Edward Robinson, 2011.

*** Check out more books by Dale Campfield at www.dalecamp-field.com ***

Don't Forget: YOUR GREATEST DAYS ARE YET AHEAD OF YOU!

You watch. . . You wait. . . You'll see!

CPSIA information can be obtained at www.ICGtesting.com
Printed in the USA
LVOW07s1941141113

361193LV00003B/5/P